QUICK QUILTS *from the* HEART

LIZ PORTER AND MARIANNE FONS

Oxmoor House®

INTRODUCTION

Quiltmakers have always used the work of their hands to express feelings. Those of us who love quilts make them because we enjoy fabric, color, and pattern. But quilts also carry messages, speaking as eloquently as words. Traditions begun long ago—of making quilts to celebrate life and love—are well maintained today.

We welcome a newborn with a quilt. When a child goes off to college, she takes a quilt. We celebrate weddings, anniversaries, and holidays by making quilts. And we show friends how much we love them with quilts.

The projects in this book are made for love. They are heart-warming quilts borrowed from other quilters and projects created for us by talented designers. And we spent many happy days with friends to cut and sew and lunch together while making quilts for this book.

Our instructions incorporate the timesaving methods we favor. You'll find rotary cutting, strip piecing, and other quick techniques. We also include instructions for traditional methods in case you prefer them.

We hope you will choose to make many projects from this collection that comes from the heart.

YOUR QUILTING FRIENDS,

Liz + Marianne

Quick Quilts from the Heart
from the *For the Love of Quilting* series

© 1994 by Liz Porter and Marianne Fons
Published by Oxmoor House, Inc., and
    Leisure Arts, Inc.

Oxmoor House, Inc.
Book Division of Southern Progress
    Corporation
P.O. Box 2463, Birmingham, Alabama 35201

Library of Congress Catalog Card
    Number: 94-67166
Hardcover ISBN: 0-8487-1433-4
Softcover ISBN: 0-8487-1442-3
Manufactured in the United States of America
Seventh Printing 1998

Editor-in-Chief: Nancy J. Fitzpatrick
Senior Crafts Editor: Susan Ramey Wright
Senior Editor, Editorial Services: Olivia K. Wells
Art Director: James Boone

QUICK QUILTS FROM THE HEART
Editor: Patricia Wilens
Editorial Assistant: Wendy L. Wolford
Copy Editor: Susan Cheatham
Copy Assistant: Jennifer K. Mathews
Designer: Melissa Jones Clark
Senior Photographer: John O'Hagan
Photostylist: Katie Stoddard
Illustrator: Kelly Davis
Production and Distribution
    Director: Phillip Lee
Production Manager: Gail Morris
Associate Production Manager: Theresa L. Beste
Production Assistant: Marianne Jordan
Publishing Systems Administrator: Rick Tucker

QUILTED WITH LOVE

The best quilts are

stitched with love.

The work of our hands

celebrates the people

in our hearts,

the milestones of our

lives, and the

comfort of friends.

Fancy Fans instructions
begin on page 14.

SPECIAL EVENTS QUILTS

Make quilts to mark the milestones in the lives of loved ones. These important events will stay fresh in their memories with reminders of fabric scraps or inscriptions.

To honor two friends, Marianne made this bright version of an old classic. **FANCY FANS** has 32 blocks, one for each year of Shirley and Gary Allen's marriage. Their names, wedding date, and hometown are embroidered on the companion **FANCY FAN PILLOW**. The friendship this quilt represents is as important to the Allens as its beauty.

Fancy Fan Pillow instructions begin on page 19.

7

Marty Freed enlisted family and friends to help make this scrap quilt to honor her daughter Emily's high school graduation. Marty sent prepared triangles of fabric to loved ones near and far so they could write out their congratulations. The signed triangles became part of the Hourglass blocks that alternate with the traditional block called **FARMER'S DAUGHTER**. The inscriptions are a jumble of joyful tributes and exuberant comments from Emily's favorite people. This pretty quilt will always be a loving memento of happy times for an Iowa farmer's daughter.

Farmer's Daughter instructions begin on page 20.

Dad's Still Not Conservative
instructions begin on page 26.

FOR THE GUYS

When a man wants a quilt that looks like a *man's* quilt, then nothing pretty or flowery will do. So the quilter who loves him will want to make a quilt with wonderfully masculine appeal to reflect the personality of that special guy.

For the man who has his own sense of style, **DAD'S STILL NOT CONSERVATIVE** is a humorous wall hanging to brighten an office or den. Use exotic fabrics to create stylish neckties or recycle real ties that he no longer wears.

Liz captured the spirit of the American Southwest in **DESERT MIRAGE**, a quilt she made for her son, Jacob. She mixed varied tan fabrics for the background and added desert colors to create a design inspired by traditional Indian motifs.

Desert Mirage **instructions
begin on page 30.**

SECRET SISTER GIFTS

Secret sisters play fairy godmother to a friend at quilting meetings. A special quilter received a basket block each month for a year, sent from her secret sister. Liz revealed her identity as the mystery friend with the last block. The blocks were set together in the **BIG SISTER BASKET** quilt.

Liz used scraps from the big project to make the **LITTLE SISTER BASKET** blocks. The wall hanging is a tribute to friendship with the addition of friends' autographs on each little basket.

Delight your secret sister with a **CHATELAINE & SEWING KIT**. Folding scissors are attached to one of the chatelaine's pockets. Add the recipient's name and the chatelaine can be worn at guild activities as a name tag. Before giving the gift, fill the pockets with needles and threads.

The matching sewing kit has plastic zip-top bags sewn inside to store sewing notions.

Little Sister Basket **instructions begin on page 35.**

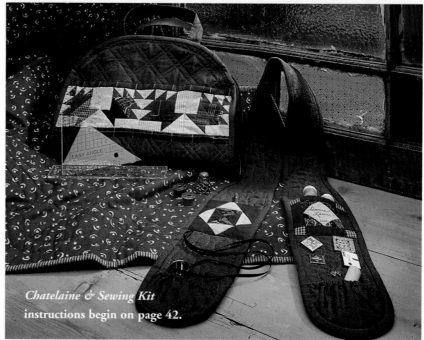

Chatelaine & Sewing Kit **instructions begin on page 42.**

Big Sister Basket instructions
begin on page 38.

FANCY FANS

You'll love the strip-piecing technique Marianne used to make two-toned blades for these fan blocks. Instructions are for 33 blocks—32 for the quilt and an extra block for a pretty toss pillow (see page 19).

Finished size of quilt: 84" x 93"   **Finished size of block:** 12" square

MATERIALS

5½ yards of white fabric

½ yard *each* of 11 dark pastel print fabrics for fans and border (Marianne used 2 pink, 2 yellow, 2 green, 2 purple, and 3 blue fabrics)

½ yard *each* of 11 light pastel print fabrics to coordinate with dark pastels listed above

¾ yard of pink fabric for bias binding

7½ yards of backing fabric or 3 yards of 90"-wide muslin

90" x 108" (queen-size) precut batting

Rotary cutter, acrylic ruler, and cutting mat

Template plastic

Plastic-coated freezer paper

CUTTING

Make templates for patterns A and B on page 17.

From white fabric, cut:

♥ 11 (12½"-wide) strips. From these, cut 33 (12½") squares for fan blocks.

♥ 1 (9⅜"-wide) strip. From this, cut 2 (9⅜") squares. Cut both squares in half diagonally to get 4 triangles for inner quilt corners. From remainder of strip, cut 2 (8½") squares for border corners.

♥ 2 (18¼"-wide) strips. From these, cut 4 (18¼") squares. Cut each square diagonally in both directions to get 14 setting triangles and 2 extra.

♥ 2 (2⅛"-wide) strips for straight-grain binding.

From *each* dark pastel fabric, cut:

♥ 4 (2"-wide) strips for fan blades.

♥ 3 (1½"-wide) strips for border.

♥ 3 B pieces, following special instructions on pattern.

From *each* light pastel fabric, cut:

♥ 4 (2"-wide) strips for fan blades.

♥ 3 (1½"-wide) strips for border.

MAKING FAN BLADES

1. Pair light and dark strips of same color (e.g., light pink with dark pink), making 11 fabric combinations—2 pink, 2 yellow, 2 green, 2 purple, and 3 blue.

2. Join strip pairs, making 44 strip sets (4 of each fabric combination). Do not open sewn strips. Leaving right sides facing, press seams flat.

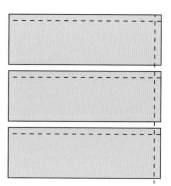

Chain Stitching Diagram

3. Cut strip sets into 8¼"-long segments to get 18 segments of each fabric combination.

4. With light fabric strip on top, stitch across 1 short end of each folded segment. To speed up sewing, chain-piece as shown in *Chain Stitching Diagram*.

5. Trim and clip sewn corners as shown in diagrams 1 and 2.

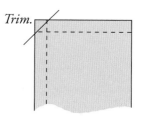

Trim.

Diagram 1

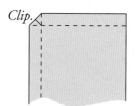

Clip.

Diagram 2

Diagram 3   *Diagram 4*

6. Open each blade, turning sewn corner right side out as shown in *Diagram 3*. Carefully insert seam ripper in tip to push out a sharp point. Press long seam allowances toward dark fabric and corner seam allowances toward light fabric as shown.

7. Place template A on *wrong* side of blade, aligning corners and center seam line as shown in *Diagram 4*. With pencil, trace template outline at sides and bottom. Trim blade on marked lines.

8. Repeat to make 198 fan blades, 6 for each block.

Making Fan Blocks

1. Select 6 matching blades for each fan. Join blades as shown in *Fan Block Diagram*.

2. Pin each pieced fan on a white background square, aligning outside raw edges of fan with sides of square.

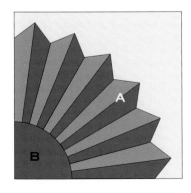

Fan Block Diagram

Designed and made by Marianne Fons for Shirley and Gary Allen of Winterset, Iowa, to celebrate their 32nd wedding anniversary, 1992. Hand-quilted by Toni Fisher.

3. For each fan, prepare a B corner piece that matches dark fabric. Turn seam allowance under at fold line on curved edge and baste.

4. Pin B piece at block corner, aligning raw edges at sides. Curved edge of B piece should cover ¼" at bottom of fan blades.

5. Hand- or machine-appliqué fan points to background square. Appliqué curved edge of B piece to fan. See General Instructions (page 168) for instructions on machine blindstitch or invisible appliqué.

6. Appliqué 32 blocks for quilt. If desired, make an extra block for a toss pillow.

7. Turn each completed block to wrong side. Trim background fabric behind fan blades and behind B piece, leaving ¼" seam allowances. Trim excess blade fabric behind fan tips, being careful not to cut top fabric.

(continued)

QUILT ASSEMBLY

1. Join blocks in diagonal rows as shown in *Quilt Assembly Diagram*. Fill in top, bottom, and sides with corner triangles and setting triangles.

2. Press seams in opposite directions from row to row. Join rows.

3. Referring to *Strip Set Diagram*, make 10 strip sets. For 5 of these, use 3 dark strips and 2 light strips, alternating light and dark fabrics as shown. For remaining 5 strip sets, use 3 light strips and and 2 dark strips.

4. From these strip sets, cut 48 (8½"-long) segments, 23 with 3 light strips and 25 with 3 dark strips.

5. For each side border, join 9 dark segments and 8 light segments, alternating from dark to light. Each

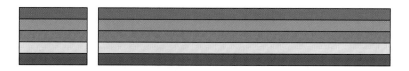

Strip Set Diagram

border will have dark segments on both ends. Join remaining 14 segments for bottom border in same manner, beginning with a dark segment and ending with a light segment.

6. Sew side borders to quilt. Press seam allowances toward inner quilt.

7. Remove 2 strips from light end of bottom border; then sew a white corner square to both ends of border. Join border to bottom of quilt. Press seam allowances toward inner quilt.

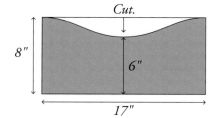

Border Curve Diagram

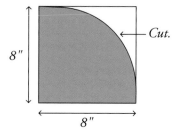

Corner Curve Diagram

MARKING BORDER CURVES

1. From freezer paper, cut 1 (8" x 17") piece and 1 (8") square.

2. Referring to *Border Curve Diagram* and *Corner Curve Diagram*, draw border and corner curves on freezer paper. Cut paper away from drawn curves as shown.

3. Pin border pattern on quilt, aligning long straight edge with border seam and 1 short edge with top edge of quilt. Lightly trace curve onto border. Reposition pattern as needed to mark 5 repeats on each side border and 4 repeats on bottom border.

4. Use corner pattern to mark curve on corner squares.

5. Do not cut curves until quilting is complete and binding is sewn to quilt top.

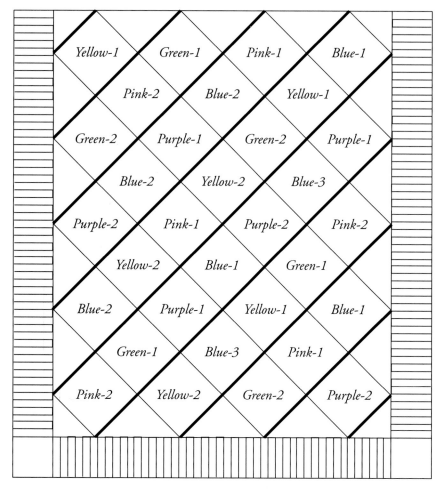

Quilt Assembly Diagram

QUILTING AND FINISHING

1. To make a pieced backing, divide backing fabric into 3 (2½-yard) lengths. Join 2 pieces lengthwise. Cut remaining piece in half lengthwise and discard 1 half. Sew narrow panel to 1 side of backing.

2. Mark desired quilting designs on quilt top. Layer backing, batting, and quilt top; baste. Backing seams will be horizontal to sides of quilt.

3. The quilt shown has flowers quilted in block corners and setting triangles, as well as outline-quilting along seams. Quilt as desired.

4. Referring to tip box on page 18, make 300" of 2"-wide *continuous bias* binding from a 27" square of pink fabric.

5. See General Instructions (page 174) for directions on making and applying binding. Align raw edge with marked curves to sew bias binding to sides and bottom of quilt.

6. Trim border to binding seam allowance. Turn folded edge of binding to quilt back and hand-finish.

7. For top edge of quilt, apply straight-grain binding. Finish binding with overlapped corners.

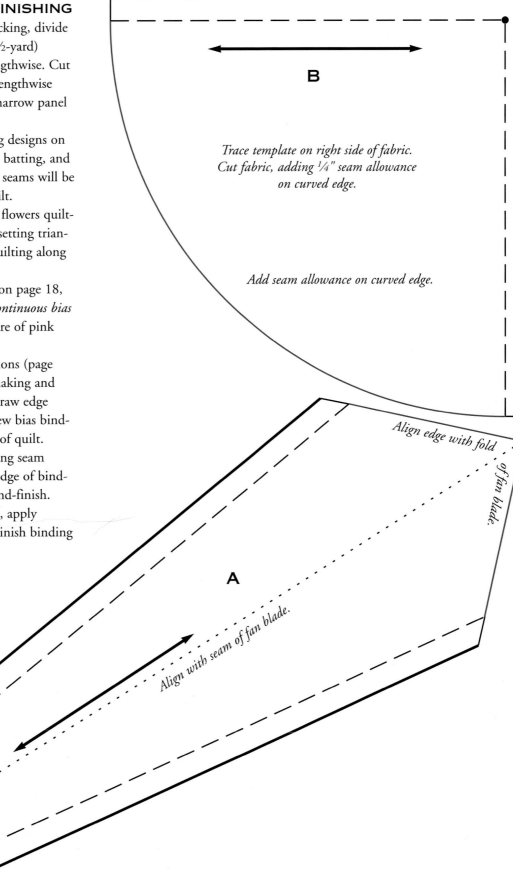

B

Trace template on right side of fabric. Cut fabric, adding ¼" seam allowance on curved edge.

Add seam allowance on curved edge.

Align edge with fold of fan blade.

A

Align with seam of fan blade.

CONTINUOUS BIAS FOR BINDING

You need a continuous strip of binding for quilts with scalloped edges such as *Fancy Fans* and *Spring Blossoms*. You can cut bias strips and join them end-to-end, but it is more efficient to make continuous binding as shown here. Start with a large square of binding fabric—project instructions will state the size of the fabric square needed.

1. Place pins at middle of each side. Position pin heads toward center of square at top and bottom edges. Point pin heads toward outside edge on remaining sides.

2. Cut square in half diagonally to get 2 triangles.

3. With right sides facing and raw edges aligned as shown, pin together edges with pin heads pointed to outside. Join with ¼" seam. Press seam *open*.

4. On wrong side of fabric, mark cutting lines parallel to long bias edges (edges without pins), spacing lines equal to width of binding strip. For example, if you need a 2"-wide binding strip, draw lines 2" apart.

5. With right sides facing and raw edges aligned, pin together edges with pin heads pointed to the inside, offsetting 1 width of binding strip. This forms a fabric tube. Join edges with ¼" seam and press seam open.

6. Begin cutting at an extended edge. Follow cutting lines, rolling tube around as you cut, until all fabric is cut in 1 continuous strip. Trim ends of strip square.

FANCY FAN PILLOW

After making the fan quilt, you can use an extra block to make a coordinating ruffled pillow. If you've made the quilt, you have enough fabric left to make one or more pillows. Materials listed below are enough to make the pillow separately.

Finished size of pillow: 15½" square, including ruffle   **Finished size of block:** 12" square

MATERIALS

¾ yard of blue-on-white print fabric for fan and outer ruffle

½ yard of white fabric for background and pillow back

¼ yard of pink fabric for inner ruffle

⅓ yard or scraps of medium blue fabric for fan

Polyester stuffing or 12"-square pillow form

Rotary cutter, acrylic ruler, and cutting mat

Template plastic

Embroidery floss and hand-sewing needle (optional)

CUTTING

Make templates for patterns A and B on page 17.

From blue-on-white print fabric, cut:

❤ 2 (2" x 25") strips for fan blades.

❤ 3 (6"-wide) strips for outer ruffle.

From white fabric, cut:

❤ 1 (12½") square for fan block.

❤ 1 (13½") square for pillow back.

From pink fabric, cut:

❤ 3 (2½"-wide) strips for inner ruffle.

From medium blue fabric, cut:

❤ 2 (2" x 25") strips for fan blades.

❤ 1 B piece.

Pillow made and embroidered by Martha Street.

MAKING FAN BLOCK

1. Sew a blue-on-white print strip to a medium blue strip, joining long edges. With right sides still facing, press seam flat just as seam was sewn. Make 2 strip sets.

2. From these strip sets, cut 6 (8¼"-long) segments.

3. To make fan blades, follow steps 4–7 on pages 14 and 15.

4. To complete block, see Making Fan Blocks on page 15.

5. Add desired embroidery on pillow front.

PILLOW ASSEMBLY

1. Join pink strips end-to-end to make 1 long strip. Repeat for blue

strips. If necessary, trim strips to same length.

2. Join ends of each strip to make loops.

3. With wrong sides facing and raw edges aligned, press each loop in half lengthwise. Pink loop is 1¼" wide after pressing and blue loop is 3" wide.

4. With raw edges aligned, place pink loop on top of blue loop. Run a gathering thread ¼" from raw edges through all layers.

5. Gather ruffle to fit pillow front. With raw edges aligned, pin ruffle on pillow front.

6. With right sides facing, pin pillow front to back, sandwiching ruffle between front and back. Stitch through all layers, leaving an opening in 1 side for turning.

7. Turn pillow right side out. Stuff with polyester stuffing. Hand-stitch opening closed.

FARMER'S DAUGHTER

The diagonal-corner technique makes quick work of 18 Farmer's Daughter blocks.
The 17 Hourglass blocks feature signatures for this commemorative quilt. See the tip box
on page 24 for advice on organizing a signature quilt project.

Finished size of quilt: 68" x 88"   **Finished size of blocks:** 10" square

MATERIALS

3½ yards of beige print fabric or
   muslin
½ yard *each* of 12 medium to dark
   green print fabrics for blocks
½ yard of golden-brown print fabric
   for inner border
¼ yard *each* of 4 dark green fabrics
   for outer border
¼ yard of light gold print fabric for
   nine-patch centers
⅛ yard *each* or scraps of at least 12
   brown, rust, and tan print fabrics
5½ yards of backing fabric or
   2¾ yards of 90"-wide muslin
81" x 96" (full-size) precut batting
Rotary cutter, acrylic ruler, and
   cutting mat
Template plastic (optional)

CUTTING

For this quilt, we used the diagonal-
corner method to make B units for
the Farmer's Daughter blocks.

If you prefer traditional cutting
and piecing methods, make templates
for patterns A, B1, and B2 on page
25. (Refer to block diagrams to identify each piece by letter.) To make a
pattern for C triangle (Hourglass
blocks), draw an 11¼" square; then
draw diagonal lines from corner to
corner in *both* directions, dividing
square into 4 C triangles. This pattern includes seam allowances.

Set aside all leftover fabrics for
pieced binding.

From beige print fabric, cut:
- 5 (5½"-wide) strips for border
  segments.
- 5 (2½"-wide) strips.
  From these, cut 72 (2½") A
  squares.
- 12 (2½"-wide) strips.
  From these, cut 72 (2½" x 6½")
  B rectangles.
- 4 (11¼"-wide) strips.
  From these, cut 11 (11¼")
  squares. Cut each square diagonally in *both* directions to get 42 C
  triangles and 2 extra. Eight triangles are for border corners. See
  page 24 for tips on how to prepare
  34 triangles for signing.

**From *each* green border fabric,
cut:**
- 2 (3½"-wide) strips.

**From *each* of 12 green print
fabrics, cut:**
- 1 (11¼") square.
  Cut this diagonally in *both* directions to get 4 C triangles.
- 3 (2½" x 21") strips.
  From these, cut 6 (2½") A squares
  for nine-patch. Then cut 12 B2
  triangles for traditional piecing *or*
  12 additional A squares for diagonal-corner piecing.

**From golden-brown print fabric,
cut:**
- 8 (1½"-wide) strips for inner
  border.

**From light gold print fabric,
cut:**
- 2 (2½" x 22") strips.
  From these, cut 18 (2½") A
  squares.

**From assorted brown, rust, and
tan scraps, cut:**
- 72 (2½") A squares.

MAKING FARMER'S DAUGHTER BLOCKS

Each Farmer's Daughter block has a
central nine-patch unit—make these
first. Then follow diagonal corner
instructions or traditional instructions
to make B units.

(continued)

*Designed and made by Marty Freed of Winterset, Iowa, in honor
of her daughter Emily's graduation from high school, 1993.*

Nine-Patch Assembly Diagram

1. Arrange 9 A squares as shown in *Nine-Patch Assembly Diagram,* using 4 green, 4 brown, and 1 light gold square.

2. Join squares in 3 rows. Press seam allowances toward brown squares.

3. Join rows to complete nine-patch. Press seam allowances away from center row.

4. To make B units with diagonal-corner technique, pin a green print A square to each end of 1 B rectangle with right sides facing as shown in *Diagonal Corner Diagram,* Figure 1. Stitch from corner to corner of each green square, making sure to angle stitching as shown. Trim squares and rectangle as shown in Figure 2, leaving ¼" seam allowance.

Figure 1

Figure 2

Diagonal Corner Diagram

Traditional B Unit Diagram

5. To make B units with traditional piecing technique, sew a green B2 triangle to each end of a beige B1 piece as shown in *Traditional B Unit Diagram.*

6. Open green triangles. Press seam allowances toward green fabric.

7. Repeat steps 1–3 to make 18 nine-patch units. Repeat steps 4 and 6 or steps 5 and 6 to make 72 B units.

8. Referring to *Farmer's Daughter Block Assembly Diagram,* arrange 1 nine-patch, 4 beige A squares, and 4 B units as shown. Join units in horizontal rows as shown; then press seam allowances toward B units. Join rows to make 1 block. Repeat to make 18 blocks.

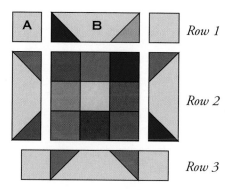

Row 1

Row 2

Row 3

*Farmer's Daughter
Block Assembly Diagram*

MAKING HOURGLASS BLOCKS

1. Combine 1 beige C triangle with a green print C triangle to make a 2-triangle unit. Make 34 units. Press seam allowances toward darker fabric.

2. Referring to *Hourglass Block Assembly Diagram,* join 2 units to make a block. Make 17 Hourglass blocks.

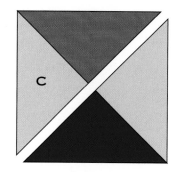

Hourglass Block Assembly Diagram

QUILT ASSEMBLY

1. Referring to *Quilt Assembly Diagram,* arrange blocks in 7 horizontal rows. Rows 1, 3, 5, and 7 have 3 Farmer's Daughter blocks and 2 Hourglass blocks, while rows 2, 4, and 6 have 2 Farmer's Daughter blocks and 3 Hourglass blocks. Heavy lines on diagram indicate inner quilt.

2. Join blocks in rows. Press seam allowances toward Hourglass blocks; then join rows.

3. Referring to *Border Strip Cutting Diagram,* measure and cut 10 border segments from 5½"-wide strips of beige fabric.

4. To piece top border, join 2 border segments and 3 green C triangles as shown in *Quilt Assembly Diagram.* Repeat for bottom border. Press seam allowances toward triangles. For each side border, join 3 border segments and 4 green triangles. Add beige C triangles to both ends of all 4 borders.

5. See General Instructions (page 169) for tips on mitered corners. Join pieced borders to inner quilt. Press seam allowances toward borders; then stitch corner seams.

6. Join strips of golden-brown fabric in pairs to make 4 long border strips.

7. Measure length of quilt top, measuring through middle of quilt rather than along sides. Trim 2 borders to this length (approximately 80½"). Sew borders to quilt sides, easing as needed. Press seam allowances toward borders.

8. Measure quilt width (including side borders), measuring through middle of quilt. Trim 2 remaining borders to this length (approximately 62½"). Join these to top and bottom edges of quilt, easing as needed. Press seam allowances toward borders.

Quilt Assembly Diagram

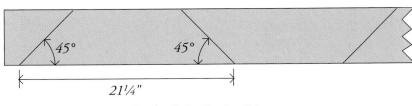

Border Strip Cutting Diagram

QUILTING AND FINISHING

1. Divide backing fabric into 2 (2¾-yard) lengths. Cut 1 piece in half lengthwise. Sew a narrow panel to each side of wide panel. Press seam allowances toward narrow panels.

2. Mark desired quilting designs on quilt top. Layer backing, batting, and quilt top; baste.

3. The quilt shown is outline-quilted along seams of patchwork; hearts are quilted in green C triangles and beige border segments. Quilt as desired.

4. To make pieced binding as shown, cut remaining fabrics into 2"-wide strips of random lengths. (You may want to cut wider strips if you used a high-loft batting.) Join strips with diagonal seams to make a continuous strip approximately 320" long. See page 174 for directions on making and applying binding.

9. For each outer border, join 2 strips of 1 green fabric end-to-end. Measure length of quilt top; trim side borders to this length (approximately 82½"). Sew borders to quilt sides.

Measure quilt width (including side borders). Trim 2 remaining borders to this length (approximately 68½"). Sew borders to top and bottom edges of quilt.

ORGANIZING A SIGNATURE QUILT

Adding written signatures, anecdotes, and memories to a quilt is a happy way to commemorate a special occasion such as a graduation or anniversary. But you should go about it in an organized manner to have the quilt ready in time for the big event.

Allow a realistic amount of time to make the quilt, and then stick to the schedule. Be as practical and conservative as you can be with your time estimates—situations always seem to come up that throw you behind schedule.

It took Marty Freed 8 weeks to plan *Farmer's Daughter*, obtain signatures, piece the top, and prepare it for quilting. To this 8 week minimum, add 2–3 weeks if you plan to machine quilt or 1–6 months for hand quilting. Here's a basic schedule for planning and executing a commemorative quilt.

Week 1
❤ Choose a block and plan the overall quilt design. The design should allow room for signatures and other writing. Marty's plan of alternating blocks allowed her to work on the Farmer's Daughter blocks while waiting for the return of the signed triangles for the Hourglass blocks.

❤ Shop for fabrics. Purchase extra of the fabric that will be used for writing so you can cut more pieces if some are not returned or are spoiled while being written on.

❤ Purchase six or more permanent pens—we recommend Sakura's Micron Pigma brand, size .01 or larger. You may need more pens if you are sending several to people far away.

❤ At an office supply store, get large envelopes for mailing fabric pieces.

Week 2
❤ Cut pieces for the quilt.

❤ Back the pieces that will be written on with plastic-coated freezer paper to make the fabric easier to write on. Cut the freezer paper to the *finished size* of each piece (without seam allowances) or slightly smaller. (For her Hourglass blocks, Marty cut 10" squares of paper in half diagonally in both directions to get four triangles.) Center and press the shiny side of the paper to the wrong side of each fabric piece.

❤ Make a list of people who you want to sign the quilt.

❤ Mail a fabric piece and a pen to each out-of-town person. Include a note explaining the project. Caution signers to write only on the paper-backed area of the fabric. (Non-sewers do not understand seam allowances!) Send an extra piece in each package in case of mistakes. Set a 1-week deadline for returning the pieces and pen—make it easy by including stamped, addressed return envelopes. Ask participants to return unused pieces with the signed ones.

Weeks 3 and 4

❤ Distribute fabric pieces and pens to local family and friends. Marty enlisted a few of Emily's friends to obtain signatures from school pals.

❤ At the end of Week 4, check the list to see whose fabric is missing. Make the necessary phone calls.

Weeks 5 and 6

❤ Remove the paper backing from the signed fabric pieces. Set the ink by pressing fabric pieces with a dry iron set at medium (cotton) heat.

❤ Begin assembling the blocks with the signed pieces you have.

❤ Check your mailbox daily for envelopes with fabric pieces. Collect signed pieces from local people who have not yet returned them.

❤ Finish making the signature blocks. Save a few blank sections for additional friends to write on later.

Weeks 7 and 8

❤ Lay out the blocks and assemble the quilt top.

❤ Piece and add the borders.

❤ Mark quilting designs.

❤ Piece the quilt back. Layer and baste the quilt.

Week 9 to Final Week

❤ Set a schedule for the quilting. Again, be realistic in your time plans—allow for interruptions. Try to do a little quilting each day.

❤ Allow a week before the big event to make and sew on the binding.

❤ Make a memory patch to sew to the back of the quilt. On it, write the date and occasion, your name, the name of the person for whom the quilt was made, and any other information you want to include.

❤ Present the gift-wrapped quilt to the special person. Be prepared for lots of tears, joy, and gratitude!

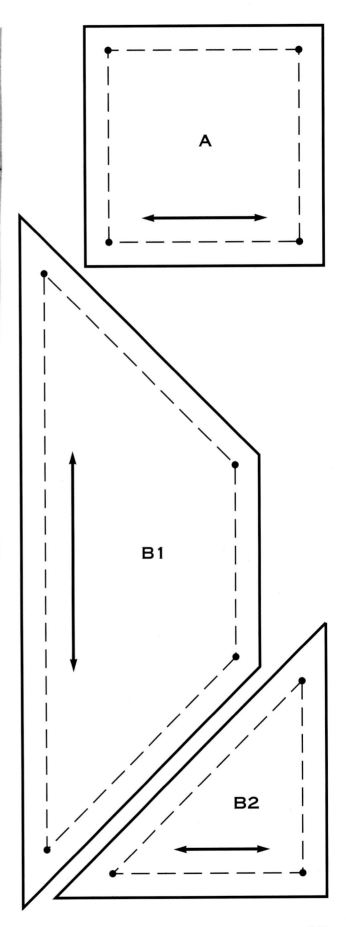

DAD'S STILL NOT CONSERVATIVE

Mix all kinds of fabrics in this humorous wall hanging, perfect for a fashion-conscious man.
Lively prints counterpoint staid checks and stripes in the 12 appliquéd shirt blocks. The pieced border of
28 Bow Tie blocks are a happy blend of plaids and polka dots.

Finished size of quilt: 40" x 40"
Finished size of shirt blocks: 6" x 8"   **Finished size of Bow Tie blocks:** 2" x 4"

MATERIALS

1 yard of red-and-black check fabric
  for outer border and binding
½ yard of black fabric for narrow
  borders
½ yard of ivory fabric for pieced border
9" x 22" piece *each* of 12 plaid, stripe,
  or check fabrics for shirts
9" x 22" piece *each* of 12 print fabrics
  for neckties
5" squares of 28 assorted fabrics for
  bow ties
45" x 60" (crib-size) precut batting
24 (³⁄₁₆"-diameter) buttons for shirts
Rotary cutter, acrylic ruler, and
  cutting mat
Template plastic or plastic-coated
  freezer paper

CUTTING

Make templates for appliqué patterns
A, B, and C on page 28. Position
templates on directional fabrics to
give each shape the desired effect.

For traditional piecing, make templates for patchwork patterns V, W,
X, Y, and Z on page 28. Even if you
are rotary cutting, you will need to
make templates for patterns W, X,
and Y and cut these pieces traditionally. Refer to block diagrams to identify each piece by letter.

From red-and-black check fabric, cut:

♥ 4 (4½"-wide) strips for outer
  borders.

From black border fabric, cut:

♥ 2 (1½" x 24½") strips.
♥ 2 (1½" x 26½") strips.
♥ 2 (1½" x 30½") strips.
♥ 2 (1½" x 32½") strips.

From ivory fabric, cut:

♥ 3 (1⅞"-wide) strips.
  From these, cut 48 (1⅞") squares.
  Cut each square in half diagonally
  to get 96 Z triangles.
♥ 2 (2⅞") squares.
  Cut each square in half diagonally
  to get 4 V triangles.
♥ 56 Y pieces.

From *each* shirt fabric, cut:

♥ 1 (6½" x 8½") piece for shirt front.
♥ 1 C and 1 C reversed for collar.

From *each* necktie fabric, cut:

♥ 1 A tie piece.
♥ 1 B knot piece.

From *each* bow tie fabric, cut:

♥ 2 X pieces.
♥ 1 W bow tie knot.
  See tip box on page 29 on marking match points for set-in seams.

MAKING SHIRT BLOCKS

1. Using your favorite appliqué
method, prepare pieces A, B, C, and
C reverse for each shirt.

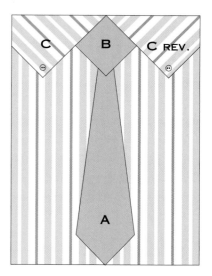

Shirt Block Diagram

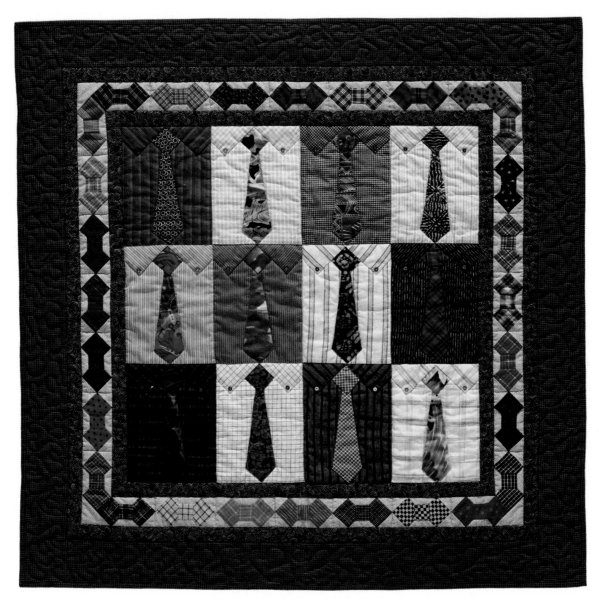

Designed and made by Nancy Graves of Manhattan, Kansas, 1993.

2. Fold shirt rectangle in half vertically, finger-pressing a crease to mark center line. Pin A piece on shirt front, aligning point with center line ¼" from bottom edge. Referring to *Shirt Block Diagram,* center and pin matching B piece ¼" from top edge of shirt front. Appliqué A and B pieces.

3. Appliqué C and C reverse pieces to shirt front. Sew a button at collar points as shown.

4. Repeat to make 12 shirt blocks.

MAKING BOW TIE BLOCKS

Note: See page 29 for tips on sewing set-in seams.

1. Referring to *Bow Tie Block Diagram,* sew matching X pieces to sides of each W square. Sew only between match points; do not sew into seam allowance at beginning and end of seams.

2. Set a Y piece into openings on remaining sides of W square, sewing only between match points. Press

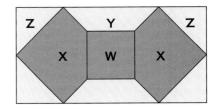

Bow Tie Block Diagram

seam allowances toward W square.

3. Add Z triangles to 4 corners of block to complete 20 Bow Tie blocks.
(continued)

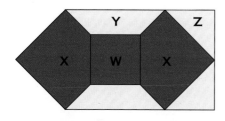

Bow Tie Corner Block Diagram

4. For border corners, make 8 more Bow Tie blocks with Z triangles on only 2 corners of block as shown in *Bow Tie Corner Block Diagram.*

QUILT ASSEMBLY

1. Referring to photograph, lay out shirt blocks in 3 horizontal rows with 4 blocks in each row. Join blocks into rows. Press seam allowances in alternate directions from row to row.

2. Join rows. Press seam allowances to 1 side.

3. Sew 24½"-long black borders to sides of quilt top; then sew 26½"-long borders to top and bottom edges. Press seam allowances toward borders.

4. Join 5 Bow Tie blocks for each of 4 pieced borders; then add a corner block to ends of each row. Press seam allowances to 1 side.

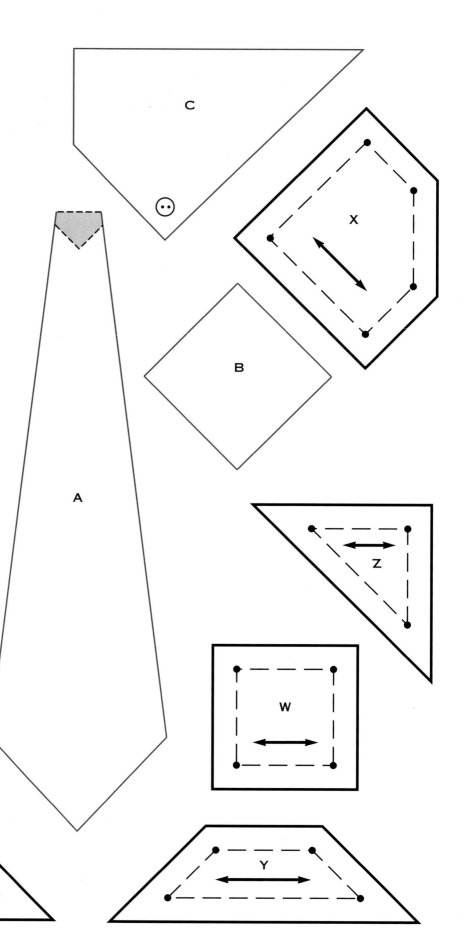

5. Join a pieced border to each side of quilt. See General Instructions (page 169) for tips on mitering corner seams.

6. Add a V triangle to each border corner. Press seam allowances toward V triangles.

7. Sew 30½"-long black borders to sides of quilt; then sew 32½"-long borders to top and bottom edges.

8. Trim 2 red-and-black border strips to 32½" long and 2 strips to 40½" long. Sew these to quilt in same manner as black borders, pressing seam allowances toward borders.

QUILTING AND FINISHING

1. Layer backing, batting, and quilt top; baste.

2. Outline-quilt along seams, collars, and neckties. Add free-style "squiggles" of quilting in outer border.

3. See General Instructions (page 174) for directions on making and applying binding. Make 180" of straight-grain binding.

4. See page 145 for directions on making a hanging sleeve.

SETTING IN PATCHWORK PIECES

Setting patchwork pieces into an opening requires more than the usual accuracy in sewing. We find the following methods helpful in this process.

1. Even if you quick-cut fabric pieces such as the squares and triangles that are set into the String Star, make plastic templates for these pieces. Mark corner points of sewing lines on each template.

2. Using a large needle (such as a used sewing machine needle) or a ⅛"-diameter hole-punch, pierce a hole in templates at each corner mark (*Diagram 1*).

3. Place template on *wrong* side of corresponding fabric piece. Mark matching points on fabric piece through template holes. Repeat on all pieces that will meet at a corner seam.

Diagram 1

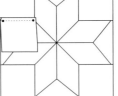

Diagram 2

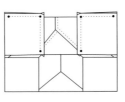

Diagram 3

4. Use matching points to align fabric pieces when pinning.

5. To join pieces that form an angled opening, sew only from dot to dot, leaving seam allowances free at beginning and end of each seam. Backstitch to secure stitching at beginning and end of each seam.

6. To set a piece into an opening between 2 other pieces, begin by pinning 1 side of it in place, using matching points as an aid. Sew pinned seam between matching points (*Diagram 2*), starting at outer edge and stopping at corner dot. Backstitch.

7. Before sewing next seam, realign fabric to pin adjacent side in place. Stitch between matching points, starting at corner dot and stopping at outside edge (*Diagram 3*).

DESERT MIRAGE

This quilt is assembled with pieced rows instead of blocks as in most quilts.
Liz quick-pieced the rows, using the diagonal-end technique (see General Instructions, page 165).
All of her fabrics are solids, but you might like to mix in a few prints.

Finished size of quilt: 58" x 84"

MATERIALS

2¼ yards of tan fabric for outer border and patchwork

¾ yard *each* of 4 coordinating tan fabrics

⅓ yard of dark green fabric for inner border

¼ yard *each* of 20 fabrics in varying shades of blue, green, teal, purple, rust, and rose

½ yard of burgundy fabric for binding

5 yards of backing fabric or 1¾ yards of 90"-wide muslin

72" x 90" (twin-size) precut batting

Rotary cutter, acrylic ruler, and cutting mat

Template plastic (optional)

CUTTING

For diagonal-end technique, cut strips and rectangles as listed below. If you prefer traditional cutting and piecing, make templates for patterns A–E on page 34. (Refer to diagrams on page 32 to identify each piece by letter.) As you cut pieces, stack and label them in groups by letter.

From tan border fabric, cut:

❤ 4 (3½" x 80") lengthwise strips for outer border.

❤ 6 (1½" x 61") lengthwise strips for sashing.

❤ 12 (1½" x 40") lengthwise strips. From these, cut 12 *each* of A (1½" x 2½"), B (1½" x 4½"), C (1½" x 6½"), D (1½" x 8½"), and E (1½" x 10½").

From *each* of 4 coordinating tan fabrics, cut:

❤ 13 (1½"-wide) strips. From strips of each fabric, cut 16 *each* of A (1½" x 2½"), B (1½" x 4½"), C (1½" x 6½"), D (1½" x 8½"), and E (1½" x 10½"). *Note:* When all tan fabrics are cut, you should have 76 *each* of pieces A, B, C, D, and E.

From dark green border fabric, cut:

❤ 7 (1½"-wide) strips for inner border.

From *each* colored fabric, cut:

❤ 4 (1½"-wide) strips. From strips of each fabric, cut 4 *each* of A (1½" x 2½"), B (1½" x 4½"), C (1½" x 6½"), D (1½" x 8½"), and E (1½" x 10½"). *Note:* When all colored fabrics are cut, you should have 78 *each* of pieces A, B, C, D, and E, plus some extras.

MAKING UNIT ROWS

Desert Mirage is pieced in long horizontal units. *Unit I* and *Unit II diagrams* show the 2 types of units. Each unit has 5 pieced rows. Choose either the diagonal-end method or traditional piecing to make rows. See General Instructions (page 165) for more information on diagonal-end technique. *(continued)*

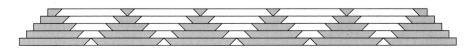

Unit I—Make 8.

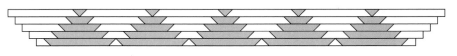

Unit II—Make 6.

Designed and made by Liz Porter for Jacob Porter, 1993. Machine-quilted by Fern Stewart.

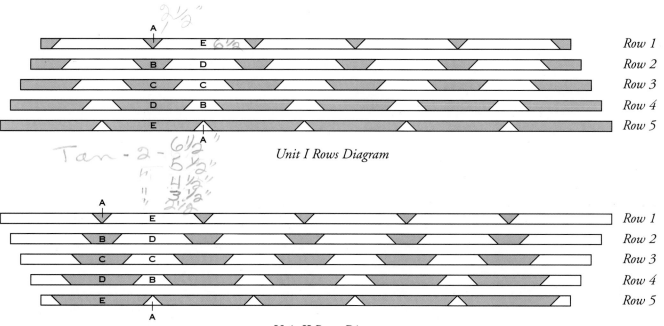

Unit I Rows Diagram

Row 1
Row 2
Row 3
Row 4
Row 5

Tan - 2 - 6½"
5½"
4½"
3½"
2½"

Unit II Rows Diagrams

Row 1
Row 2
Row 3
Row 4
Row 5

1. Referring to *Unit I Rows Diagram,* lay out pieces for each row. Each row has 5 tan pieces and 6 colored pieces.

2. Begin making Row 1 from right end. With right sides facing, position a tan E piece at 1 end of a colored A piece as shown in *Diagram 1.*

3. To join pieces, stitch diagonally from corner to corner, angling seam as shown. Trim seam allowance to ¼" and press toward darker fabric. Right side of pieced unit should look like *Diagram 2.*

4. With right sides facing, position a colored A piece at unsewn end of tan E piece. Join pieces as before, angling seam as shown in *Diagram 3.* Trim and press seam allowances. Right side of pieced unit should look like *Diagram 4.*

5. Referring to diagrams 1–6 and *Unit I Rows Diagram,* continue to join A and E pieces in this manner to make Row 1 as shown.

6. Referring to *Unit I Rows Diagram,* make rows 2–5 in same manner.

7. In each completed row, fold all

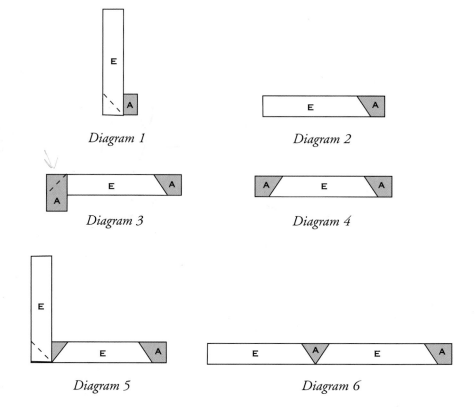

Diagram 1

Diagram 2

Diagram 3

Diagram 4

Diagram 5

Diagram 6

tan pieces in half and lightly crease. Pin rows together, aligning creases on tan pieces. Join rows to complete Unit I.

8. Make 8 of Unit I.

9. In a similar manner, make 6 of Unit II. There are 6 tan pieces and 5 colored pieces in each row. Refer to *Unit II Rows Diagram* for correct pieces and sequence in each row.

32

Quilt Assembly

1. Referring to *Quilt Assembly Diagram,* lay out units and 1½" x 61" tan sashing strips on floor.

2. Fold E and A pieces in half at unit edges and crease. As you join units, match creases to align. Join units and tan strips in sequence shown in *Quilt Assembly Diagram.* Press seam allowances toward tan strips when possible.

3. To trim quilt sides as indicated by lines on diagram, align edge of ruler with center of side A pieces; then move ruler ¼" toward quilt edge to add seam allowance. Trim excess fabric on this line.

4. For each side inner border, join 2 green strips end-to-end. Cut 1 remaining border strip in half. For top and bottom borders, join a half strip to each remaining border strip.

5. Measure length of quilt through middle of quilt. Trim side borders to this length (approximately 76½"). Sew borders to quilt sides. Press seam allowances toward borders.

6. Measure width of quilt in same manner. Trim remaining green borders to this length (approximately 52½"). Sew borders to top and bottom edges of quilt. Press seam allowances toward borders.

7. Add tan border strips to quilt in same manner.

Quilting and Finishing

1. Divide backing fabric into 2 (2½-yard) lengths. Cut 1 piece in half lengthwise. Sew 1 narrow panel to 1 side of wide panel. Press seam allowances toward narrow panel.

2. Mark desired quilting designs on patchwork. The quilt shown has a traditional squash blossom design in colored medallions (see pattern on page 34) and a half blossom in colored zigzags. A pattern is also given

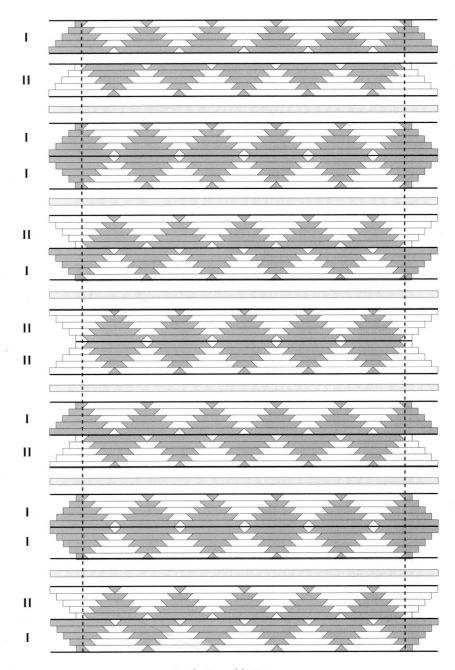

Quilt Assembly Diagram

for single cable quilted in border. Mark parallel diagonal lines through tan zigzags.

3. Layer backing, batting, and quilt top; baste.

4. Quilt marked designs as desired.

5. See General Instructions (page 174) for directions on making and applying binding. Make 300" of straight-grain binding.

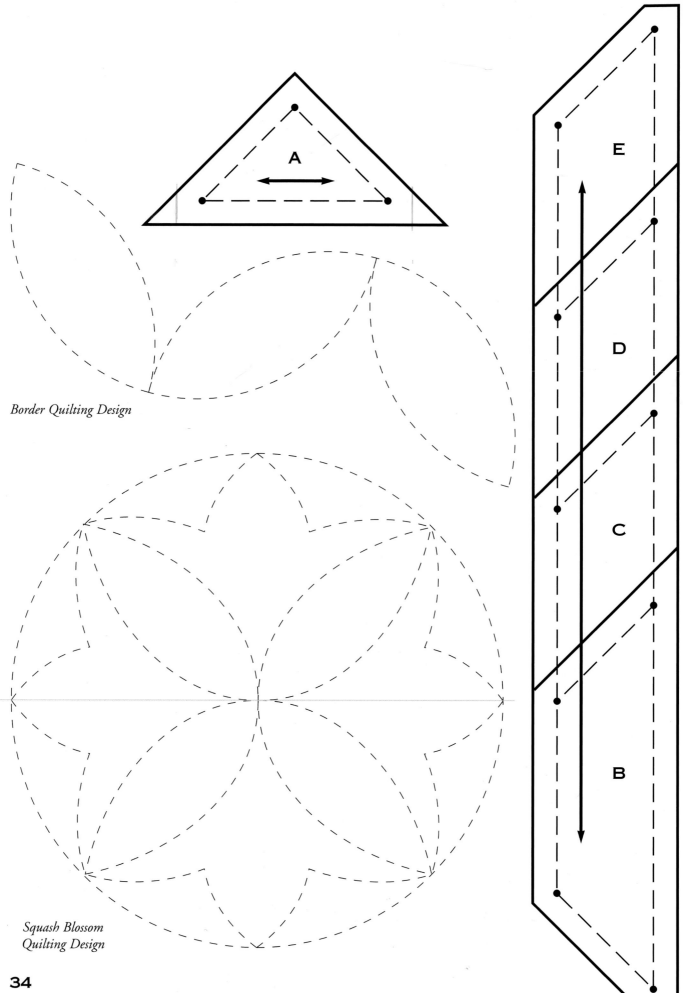

A

E

D

C

B

Border Quilting Design

Squash Blossom
Quilting Design

LITTLE SISTER BASKET

Some friends signed fabric scraps that Liz used to personalize 12 cheery baskets. Made entirely of fabrics left over from other projects, this little wall hanging is the ideal weekend project. It's a quick gift to show longlasting friendship.

Finished size of quilt: 21" x 26½"   **Finished size of block:** 4" square

MATERIALS

¾ yard of blue print fabric for setting
    pieces and binding

½ yard of cream print fabric

¼ yard of black print fabric for
    borders

7" square *each* of 12 print fabrics for
    baskets

¾ yard of backing fabric

26" x 31" piece of low-loft batting

Rotary cutter, acrylic ruler, and
    cutting mat

Template plastic (optional)

CUTTING

Refer to diagram on page 36 to identify each piece by letter. For traditional cutting, make templates for shaded patterns A–D on page 37.

From blue print fabric, cut:

❤ 1 (4½"-wide) strip.
    From this, cut 6 (4½") setting
    squares.

❤ 4 (2½") squares for border corners.

❤ 1 (7"-wide) strip.
    From this, cut 3 (7") squares and
    2 (3¾") squares. Cut each 7"
    square diagonally in *both* directions to get 10 setting triangles
    and 2 extra. Cut each 3¾" square
    in half diagonally to get 4 corner
    setting triangles.

❤ 3 (2"-wide) strips for binding.

From black print fabric, cut:

❤ 3 (2½"-wide) border strips.

From cream print fabric, cut:

❤ 1 (2⅞"-wide) strip.
    From this, cut 12 (2⅞") squares.
    Cut each square in half diagonally
    to get 24 A triangles.

❤ 2 (1½"-wide) strips.
    From this, cut 12 (1½") C squares
    and 24 (1½" x 2½") D rectangles.

❤ 2 (1⅞"-wide) strips.
    From these, cut 24 (1⅞") squares.
    Cut each square in half diagonally
    to get 48 B triangles.   *(continued)*

*Designed and made by Liz Porter and Marianne Fons, 1993.
Hand-quilted by Mary B. Larson.*

From each basket fabric, cut:

- ❤ 1 (2⅞") square. Cut square in half diagonally to get 1 A triangle and 1 extra.
- ❤ 3 (1⅞") squares. Cut squares in half diagonally to get 6 B triangles.

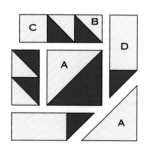

Block Assembly Diagram

MAKING BASKET BLOCKS

Press seam allowances toward darker fabric throughout except as noted. Make 12 basket blocks.

1. Referring to *Block Assembly Diagram,* select pieces for 1 block.

2. Join cream and print A triangles to make a triangle-square.

3. Join cream and print B triangles to make 4 triangle-squares.

4. Join 2 B triangle-squares in a row as shown at left of *Block Assembly Diagram.* Sew row to side of A triangle-square as shown. Press seam allowances toward A triangle.

5. Join remaining B triangle-squares to make a row as shown at top of diagram (note that dark triangles point in opposite direction from first row). Join C square to end of row. Sew row to top of A triangle-square as shown. Press seam allowances toward A.

6. Join B triangles to ends of D rectangles. Sew DB units to block sides as shown. Press seam allowances toward DB units.

7. Add cream A triangle to complete block.

QUILT ASSEMBLY

1. Referring to *Quilt Assembly Diagram,* arrange blocks, setting squares, setting triangles, and corner triangles in diagonal rows. Heavy lines on diagram indicate rows.

2. Join blocks in diagonal rows. Press seam allowances toward setting pieces.

3. Join rows as shown in diagram.

4. Measure length of quilt top through middle of quilt. Trim 2 border strips to this length (approximately 23"). Sew borders to quilt sides. Press seam allowances toward borders.

5. Measure width of quilt top in same manner. From remaining border strip, cut 2 borders this length (approximately 17⅜"). Join corner squares to ends of border strips and press seam allowances toward borders. Sew borders to top and bottom edges of quilt.

QUILTING AND FINISHING

1. Mark desired quilting designs. Use a 3"-diameter circular design for setting squares and a 1"-wide scroll or cable design for borders.

2. Layer backing, batting, and quilt top; baste. Outline-quilt patchwork and marked designs.

3. See General Instructions (page 174) for directions on making and applying binding. Make 108" of straight-grain binding.

4. See page 145 for directions on making a hanging sleeve.

Quilt Assembly Diagram

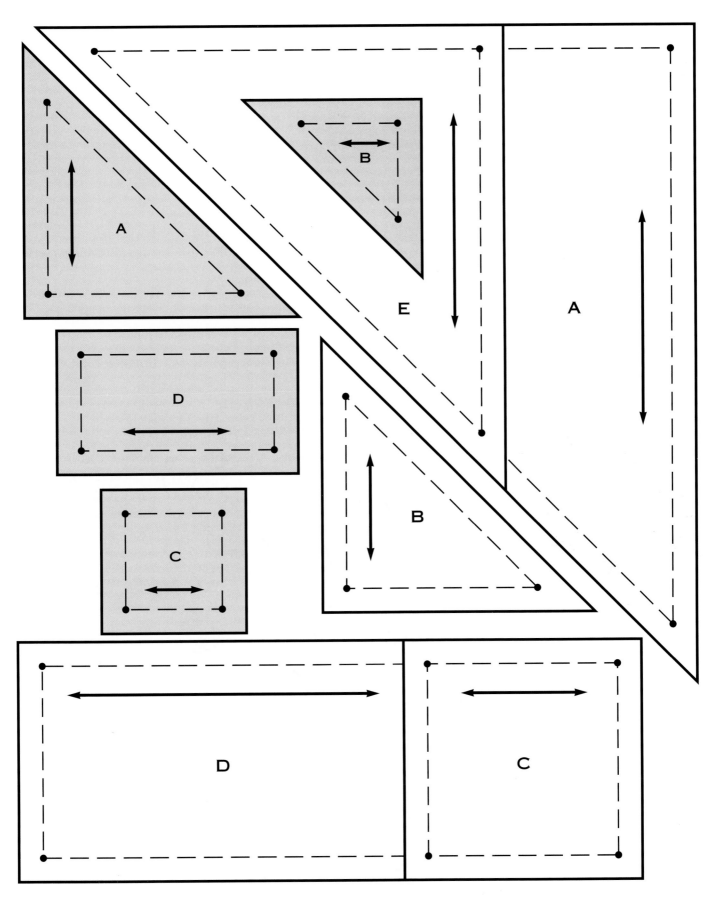

Shaded patterns are for Little Sister Basket. White patterns are for Big Sister Basket.

BIG SISTER BASKET

The traditional name of this basket block is Cake Stand. Liz and Marianne used scraps of favorite fabrics to make 15 blocks for a secret sister friendship exchange. They rotary-cut all the basket triangles from squares (see General Instructions, page 161).

Finished size of quilt: 53⅜" x 81⅝"   **Finished size of block:** 10" square

MATERIALS

2¼ yards of blue print fabric for setting pieces and binding
1½ yards of cream print fabric
1¼ yards of black print fabric for border
8" x 14" *each* of 15 print fabrics for baskets
3½ yards of backing fabric or 1¾ yards of 90"-wide muslin
72" x 90" (twin-size) precut batting
Rotary cutter, acrylic ruler, and cutting mat
Template plastic (optional)

CUTTING

Refer to block diagram to identify each piece by letter. For traditional cutting, make templates for patterns A–E on page 37.

From black print fabric, cut:
- ❤ 6 (6"-wide) border strips.

From blue print fabric, cut:
- ❤ 7 (2"-wide) strips for straight-grain binding.
- ❤ 2 (10½"-wide) strips. From these, cut 8 (10½") setting squares.
- ❤ 2 (15⅜"-wide) strips. From these, cut 3 (15⅜") squares. Cut each square diagonally in *both* directions to get 12 setting triangles.
- ❤ 1 (8"-wide) strip. From this, cut 2 (8") squares and 4 (6") squares for border corners. Cut each 8" square in half diagonally to get 4 corner setting triangles.

From cream print fabric, cut:
- ❤ 2 (6⅞"-wide) strips. From these, cut 8 (6⅞") squares. Cut each square in half diagonally to get 15 A triangles and 1 extra.
- ❤ 4 (2⅞"-wide) strips. From these, cut 45 (2⅞") squares. Cut each square in half diagonally to get 90 B triangles.
- ❤ 1 (2½"-wide) strip. From this, cut 15 (2½") C squares.
- ❤ 5 (2½"-wide) strips. From these, cut 30 (2½" x 6½") D rectangles.
- ❤ 1 (4⅞"-wide) strip. From this, cut 8 (4⅞") squares. Cut each square in half diagonally to get 15 E triangles and 1 extra.

From *each* basket fabric, cut:
- ❤ 1 (6⅞") square. Cut this in half to get 1 A triangle and 1 extra.
- ❤ 4 (2⅞") squares. Cut squares in half diagonally to get 8 B triangles.

MAKING BASKET BLOCKS

Press seam allowances toward darker fabric throughout, except as noted. Make 15 basket blocks.

1. Referring to *Basket Block Diagram,* select pieces for 1 block.

2. Join cream and print A triangles to make a triangle-square.

3. Join cream and print B triangles to make 6 triangle-squares.

(continued)

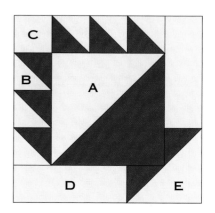

Basket Block Diagram

Designed and made by Liz Porter and Marianne Fons, 1993. Machine-quilted by Fern Stewart.

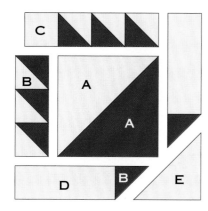

Block Assembly Diagram

4. Join 3 B triangle-squares in a row as shown at left of *Block Assembly Diagram.* Sew row to side of A triangle-square as shown. Press seam allowances toward A triangle.

5. Join remaining B triangle-squares to make a row as shown at top of diagram (note that dark triangles point in opposite direction from first row). Join C square to end of row. Press seam allowances toward C square. Sew row to top of A triangle-square as shown. Press seam allowances toward A triangle.

6. Join B triangles to ends of D rectangles. Sew DB units to block sides as shown. Press seam allowances toward DB units.

7. Add E triangle to complete block. Press seam allowance toward E triangle.

QUILT ASSEMBLY

1. Referring to *Quilt Assembly Diagram,* arrange blocks, setting squares, setting triangles, and corner triangles in diagonal rows. Heavy lines on diagram indicate rows.

2. Join blocks and setting pieces in diagonal rows. Press seam allowances toward setting pieces.

3. Join rows as shown in diagram.

4. For each side border, join 2 black strips end-to-end.

Quilt Assembly Diagram

5. Measure length of quilt through middle of quilt. Trim side borders to this length (approximately 71⅛"). Sew borders to quilt sides. Press seam allowances toward borders.

6. Measure width of quilt in same manner. Trim remaining border strips to this length (approximately 43"). Join corner squares to ends of border strips. Press seam allowances toward borders. Sew borders to top and bottom edges of quilt.

QUILTING AND FINISHING

1. Divide backing fabric into 2 (1¾-yard) lengths. Cut 1 piece in half lengthwise. Sew a narrow panel to each side of wide panel. Press seam allowances toward narrow panels.

2. Mark desired quilting designs on quilt top. A pattern for feathered quilting motif used in setting pieces is given at right. The quilt shown also has a scroll border design and vertical lines quilted through each basket.

3. Layer backing, batting, and quilt top; baste. (Backing seams will parallel top and bottom quilt edges.) Quilt as desired.

4. See General Instructions (page 174) for directions on making and applying binding. Make 285" of straight-grain binding.

Quilting Design for Big Sister Basket Quilt

Half of Pattern

CHATELAINE & SEWING KIT

Notions travel safely and conveniently in this charming chatelaine and sewing kit. Worn around the neck, the chatelaine keeps needles and thread handy but leaves hands free. The sewing kit, which can be made from a purchased quilted place mat, features stitched-in plastic zip-top bags for storing sewing supplies.

Finished size of chatelaine: Approximately 42" long   **Finished size of sewing kit:** Approximately 9" x 12¼"

CHATELAINE MATERIALS

½ yard of navy print fabric
Scraps of print fabrics for block
    pockets
⅝ yard of ⅛"-wide navy ribbon
¼ yard of ¼"-wide elastic
4½" x 44" of polyester fleece
Rotary cutter, acrylic ruler, and
    cutting mat
Freezer paper
Fold-up embroidery scissors
Fine-point permanent marker

CHATELAINE CUTTING

Trace chatelaine pattern (page 43) onto freezer paper, extending neck as indicated. To make pattern for pouch pockets, draw a 5"-diameter circle. (A saucer or plastic container may be the right size for a circle template.)

From navy print fabric, cut:

❤ 2 (4½"-wide) strips.
❤ 1 (9" x 24") piece for binding.
❤ 2 (3½") squares for block pocket
    linings.
❤ 2 (5"-diameter) circles for pouch
    pockets.

CHATELAINE ASSEMBLY

1. Layer fleece between navy print strips and baste. Machine-quilt as desired. Using paper pattern, cut chatelaine from quilted fabric.

2. For pouch pocket, fold a fabric circle in half with wrong sides facing. Stitch ⅜" from folded edge to form a casing. Cut 3½" of elastic and insert in casing. Secure elastic ends. Run gathering stitches along bottom, ⅛" from curved edge, and gather. Baste pocket to 1 end of chatelaine as shown on pattern. Repeat to make pouch pocket for opposite side.

3. For block pockets, select 1 or 2 blocks from Bonus 3" Blocks section (page 78). Choose a block like Album Patch, which has space to write on so that the block can be a personalized name tag. Following those instructions, use scraps to make 2 blocks. Use permanent pen to write on block.

4. With right sides facing, match blocks with lining squares. Stitch top and bottom edges only. Turn pockets

right side out and press. Pin pockets on chatelaine with bottom edge approximately 4" above pouch pocket.

5. Thread ribbon through 1 handle of scissors. Place ribbon ends under right pocket if user is right-handed or under left pocket if user is left-handed. Topstitch bottoms and sides of pockets to chatelaine, catching ribbon in stitching.

6. Referring to tip box on page 18, make 100" of 2½"-wide *continuous bias* binding. See General Instructions (page 174) for directions on making and applying binding.

SEWING KIT MATERIALS

¾ yard of navy print fabric*
Scraps of print fabrics for blocks
24"-long separating plastic zipper
2 yards of 1"-wide grosgrain ribbon
14" x 22" of polyester fleece*
4 each of sandwich- and gallon-size
    zip-top freezer bags
2 jewelry-size zip-top plastic bags
    (optional)
Rotary cutter, acrylic ruler, and
    cutting mat
Freezer paper
*Note: For a quicker sewing kit, substitute a 12" x 18" prequilted oval place mat for navy fabric and fleece, and add ⅔ yard of 1"-wide ribbon for handles.   *(continued)*

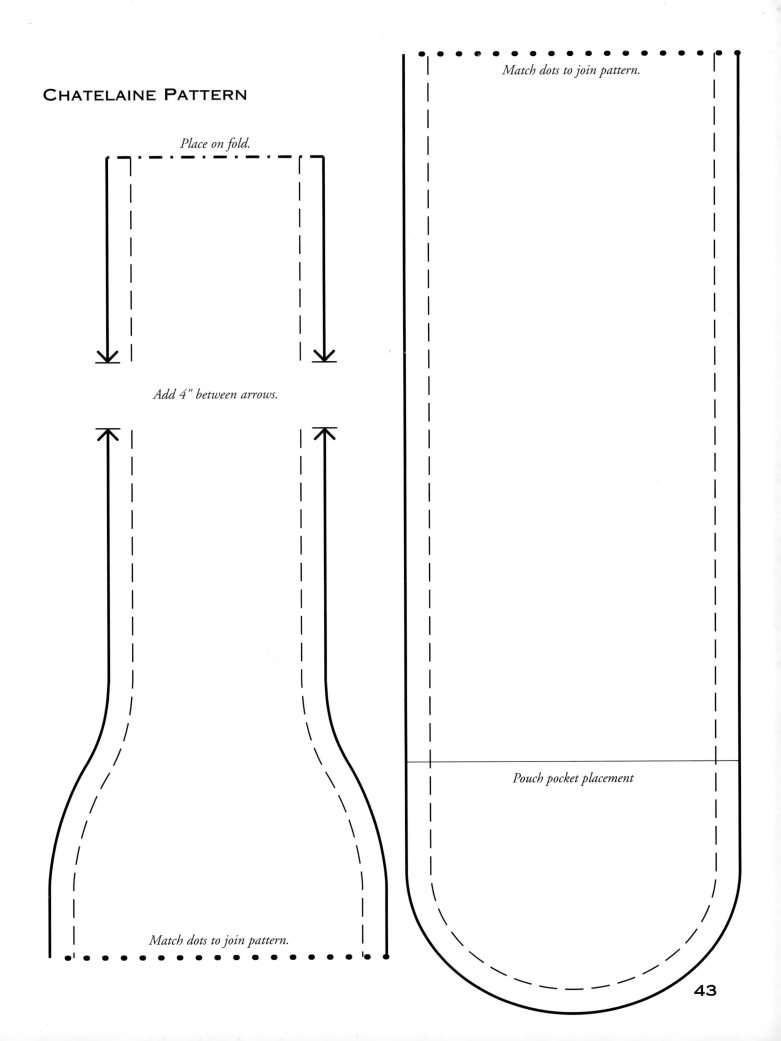

CHATELAINE PATTERN

Place on fold.

Add 4" between arrows.

Match dots to join pattern.

Match dots to join pattern.

Pouch pocket placement

43

SEWING KIT CUTTING

Fold a 20" square of freezer paper in quarters. Aligning fold lines of each quarter with straight sides of pattern on page 45, trace a full-size pattern.

From navy print fabric, cut:

- ❤ 1 (12½") square for binding.
- ❤ 2 (14" x 22") pieces for kit.
- ❤ 2 (2¼" x 11") pieces for handles.

From scraps, cut:

- ❤ 2 (1½" x 12½") pieces for block row borders.

SEWING KIT ASSEMBLY

1. Layer fleece between kit pieces and baste. Machine-quilt as desired.

2. Using paper pattern, cut kit from quilted fabric. Mark block and handle placement lines. Fold kit in half to find and mark center line indicated on pattern.

3. Select 1–4 blocks from Bonus 3" Blocks section (page 78). Following those instructions, use scraps to make 4 blocks. Join blocks in a row (see photo on page 12).

4. With wrong sides facing, press borders in half lengthwise. With raw edges aligned, sew borders to top and bottom edges of block row. Press seam allowances toward borders.

5. Topstitch block row to front of kit, sewing along folded edge of borders.

6. See General Instructions (page 174) for directions on making and applying binding. Make 60" of 2½"-wide *bias* binding. Bind edges of kit.

7. On 1 handle strip, turn ¼" to wrong side on both long edges and press. With wrong sides facing, fold strip in half and topstitch both long edges. Repeat for second handle strip. Tack handles in place on wrong side of kit.

Designed and made by Donna Larson of Johnston, Iowa, 1994.

8. Separate zipper. Cut 2 (28"-long) ribbon pieces and place 1 piece along-side each zipper tape, overlapping edges slightly. Leaving 1" of ribbon extending at both ends of each zipper tape, topstitch ribbon in place.

9. Rejoin zipper. With zipper teeth to outside of kit and placing zipper stops over center line, pin outside edges of ribbon to *wrong* side of kit just below binding as shown in *Sewing Kit Diagram*. Separate zipper and zigzag-stitch halves in place along ribbon edge, covering handle ends.

10. Lay kit flat. Layer zip-top bags inside kit on both sides of center line, with bag bottoms extending over line.

11. Cut 14" of ribbon and turn under ¾" at each end. Pin ribbon on center line of kit, on top of bags.

Tuck extra zipper ribbon under ends of center ribbon.

12. Topstitch all sides of center ribbon through all layers. Trim bag bottoms that extend past sides of ribbon.

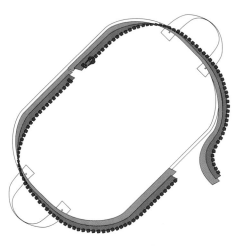

Sewing Kit Diagram

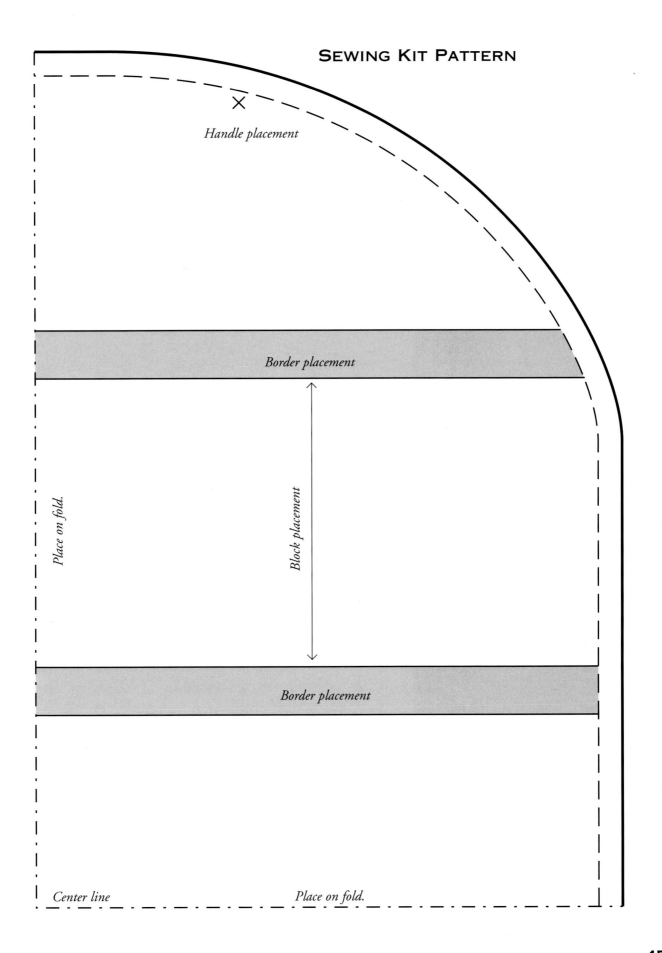

Handle placement

Border placement

Place on fold.

Block placement

Border placement

Center line

Place on fold.

QUILTING WITH FRIENDS

Share the joys of

quiltmaking with others

by combining efforts to

make a quilt quickly.

Block parties, cutting bees,

and round robin quilts

are among the many

ways for friends to

work together and for

quilts to go from

friend to friend.

Can't See the Forest for the Trees
instructions begin on page 56.

BLOCK PARTIES

Quilters know the best way to thank another quilter is to make something for her. Many guilds observe the tradition of giving blocks to retiring officers.

At the end of her term as president, North Dakota quilter Clare Degerness received a forest of string-pieced pine and maple trees. **CAN'T SEE THE FOREST FOR THE TREES** includes a community of house blocks that Clare scattered among the trees as she set this memory quilt together.

Members of the Des Moines Area Quilters' Guild made Wedding Ring blocks for outgoing officer Marilyn Parks. Marilyn put her heart into **VALLEY JUNCTION**, creating an imaginative set that allows space for elaborate feather quilting.

Valley Junction instructions begin on page 61.

Liz's Super Star instructions begin on page 65.

50

Corn and Beans instructions begin on page 70.

SHARE THE FUN

Cutting is rarely anybody's favorite part of quiltmaking. Liz and Marianne make it fun by doing it with friends.

A cutting bee is a delightful way to trade scrap fabrics and get pieces cut, sharing gossip and goodies while you work together.

LIZ'S SUPER STAR and **CORN AND BEANS** are the results of two such cutting bees. Everyone in the group cuts strips and pieces of the same size, and then creates their own quilt designs. Although everyone has shared the same fabrics, each quilt is unique.

FRIENDSHIP SAMPLERS

Trading blocks is how six Indiana friends created sampler quilts that are both the same and different.

Each woman brought six identical 3"-square blocks to monthly meetings and left with six different blocks. At year's end, everyone had 72 blocks. The challenge was to create an interesting set and have the quilt finished in time for the local quilt show.

Alternating blocks create diagonal chains of scrap fabrics in Carol Hopkins' **WITH A LITTLE HELP FROM MY FRIENDS**, a quilt ideal for quick piecing.

Connie Culverhouse's **FRIENDS TO FRIENDS** showcases the same collection of blocks in a classic diagonal set.

To start your own block-swapping project, choose from 44 blocks in our Bonus 3" Blocks section beginning on page 78.

With a Little Help from My Friends
instructions begin on page 73.

Friends to Friends instructions begin on page 76.

String Star **instructions begin on page 86.**

ROUND ROBIN CHALLENGE

A circle of friends can share creativity as well as sewing by making round robin quilts. Each person makes a central block and then passes it to other members, who add borders or other embellishments to complete the wall hanging.

Liz's group started with blocks 12"–20" square. The quilt tops passed successively to three other members, each person adding another border. Liz string-pieced a star block, which her friends embellished with one border after another. The climax of this **STRING STAR** wall hanging is a folk-art appliquéd border, buttonhole-stitched by machine.

Some round robin groups increase the challenge by setting rules for each round of borders. Create your own challenge, sharing the joy of making quilts with friends.

CAN'T SEE THE FOREST FOR THE TREES

This string-pieced forest puts narrow fabric scraps to good use. Sewing on freezer-paper foundations, make 46 pines and 12 maples to surround 14 house blocks. All but three house pieces can be quick-cut for an easy-to-make quilt that combines quick methods with traditional piecing.

Finished size of house block: 10" square **Finished size of tree blocks:** 8" x 10"
Finished size of quilt: 79" x 101"

MATERIALS
5 yards of muslin
1 yard *each* of 4 paisley fabrics for borders and houses
1 yard of dark brown fabric for chimneys, tree trunks, and binding
½ yard of light brown fabric for roofs
Scraps of dark blue and green fabrics for doors and windows
Narrow strips of assorted green and brown fabrics for pines
Narrow strips of assorted rust, yellow, and orange fabrics for maples
6 yards of backing fabric or
   3 yards of 90"-wide muslin
90" x 108" (queen-size) precut batting
Rotary cutter, acrylic ruler, and cutting mat
Plastic-coated freezer paper
2 sheets of 8½" x 11" graph paper
Template plastic (optional)

CUTTING
Cutting instructions are for rotary cutting, except for roof section of house blocks. Make plastic or freezer-paper templates for patterns H, I, and J on page 59. Refer to block diagrams to identify each piece by letter. For tree blocks, see directions for making tree blocks to make freezer-paper templates for each block.

From muslin, cut:
❤ 1 (2½"-wide) strip.
   From this, cut 4 (2½" x 10½") spacer strips.
❤ 8 (4"-wide) strips for tree trunk strip sets.
❤ 1 (1¾"-wide) strip for chimney strip set (K).
❤ 1 (4½"-wide) strip.
   From this, cut 14 (3" x 4½") L rectangles.
❤ 2 (2½"-wide) strips.
   From these, cut 28 (2½" x 3") M rectangles.
❤ 14 *each* of J and J reversed.
   Set aside remaining muslin to cut X, Y, and Z pieces for tree blocks, 1 block at a time as described in instructions for tree blocks.

From light brown fabric, cut:
❤ 7 H pieces and 7 H reversed.

From paisley fabrics, cut:
❤ 3 (6"-wide) strips from *each* of 2 fabrics for side borders.
❤ 2 (6"-wide) strips from *each* of 2 fabrics for top and bottom borders.
❤ 14 (4½" x 21") strips from assorted fabrics for house blocks. From *each* strip, cut 1 of I template, 2 (1¾" x 3¾") B rectangles, 1 (2" x 2¾") C rectangle, 2 (1½" x 2¾") E rectangles, 1 (1½" x 6½") F rectangle, and 1 (1¼" x 10½") G rectangle.

From dark brown fabric, cut:
❤ 1 (1¾"-wide) strip for chimney strip set (K).
❤ 4 (1½"-wide) strips for tree trunk strip sets.
❤ 9 (2¼"-wide) strips for binding.

From blue and green scraps, cut:
❤ 14 (2" x 3¾") A rectangles.
❤ 28 (1¾" x 2¾") D rectangles, cutting 2 matching pieces for each house.

(continued)

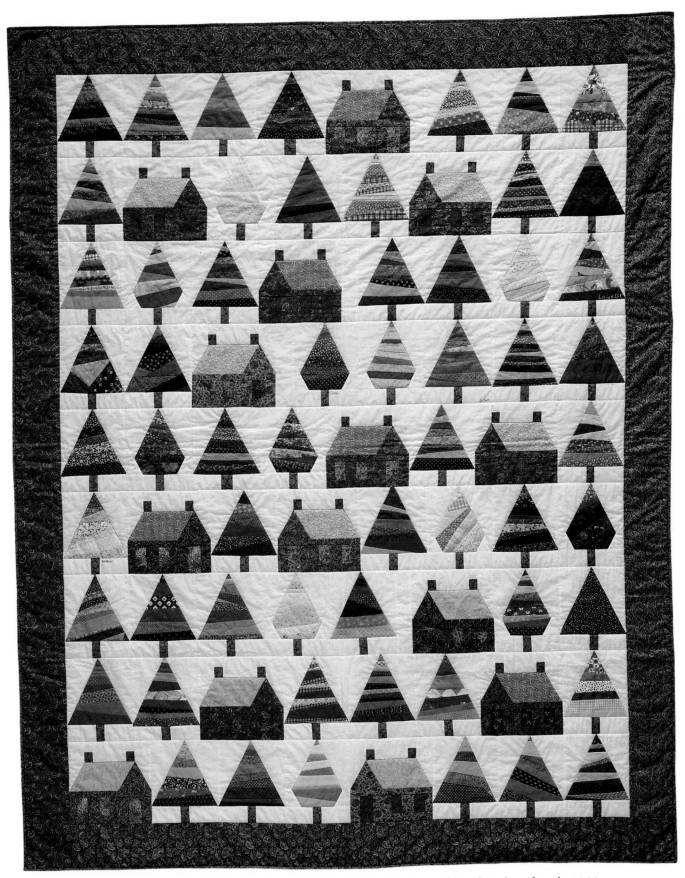

Designed and made by Clare Degerness of Moorhead, Minnesota, and North Dakota friends, 1990.

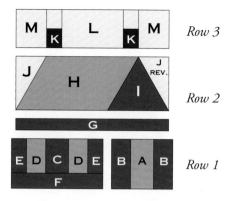

Row 3

Row 2

Row 1

House Block Assembly Diagram

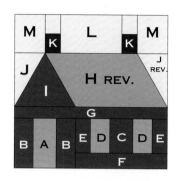

Reversed House Block Diagram

MAKING HOUSE BLOCKS

1. Referring to *House Block Assembly Diagram,* select pieces for 1 house block.

2. For door section, join B rectangles to both sides of A rectangle. Press seam allowances toward B pieces.

3. For window section, join D rectangles to both sides of C rectangle. Add E rectangles to side of each D. Press seam allowances toward D pieces. Sew F rectangle to bottom of row as shown. Press seam allowances toward F.

4. Join door and window sections as shown. Sew G rectangle to top edge to complete Row 1. Press seam allowances toward G.

5. For Row 2, join H, I, J, and J reversed pieces as shown. Press seam allowances toward dark fabrics.

6. Referring to *Chimney Strip Set Diagram,* join strips of muslin and dark brown fabric. Press seam allowances toward brown fabric. From this strip set, cut 28 (1½"-wide) K segments as shown.

Chimney Strip Set Diagram

7. Referring to Row 3 of *House Block Assembly Diagram,* join 1 L rectangle, 2 K chimney segments, and 2 M rectangles as shown.

8. Join 3 rows to complete block.

9. Make 7 blocks as shown in assembly diagram. Make 7 more blocks as shown in *Reversed House Block Diagram,* using H reversed roof pieces.

MAKING PINE TREES

1. Referring to *Pine Tree Diagram,* draw master pattern on graph paper.

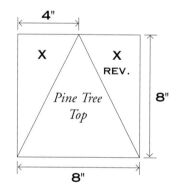

Pine Tree Diagram

2. With shiny side down, lay freezer paper over master pattern and trace pattern onto freezer paper. Cut out freezer-paper patterns for X, X reversed, and tree top.

3. Set iron on wool setting and no steam. With shiny side of paper against *wrong* side of fabric, press X and X reversed patterns onto muslin. Leave at least ½" between patterns on fabric for seam allowances. With ruler ¼" from paper edges, cut out muslin pieces with rotary cutter. (Leave paper patterns on pieces during construction until after blocks are joined.)

4. To string-piece tree top, work with shiny side of paper pattern face-up. With right side up, pin a strip of tree fabric at top of tree. Strip must be big enough to go across pattern and extend ¼" at top and sides.

5. With right sides facing, place next strip on top of first one, aligning raw edges at bottom of first strip. Stitch ¼" from aligned edges, sewing through paper. Open out top piece and finger-press.

6. Referring to *String Piecing Diagram,* continue to add strips until paper pattern is covered. Slant strips and/or cut them so widths are not uniform. Choose strips that contrast in value. Be sure strips extend at least ¼" beyond paper pattern at sides.

7. Turn tree top over to wrong side. Aligning ruler ¼" from edge of paper, use rotary cutter to trim excess fabric, leaving ¼" for seam allowances.

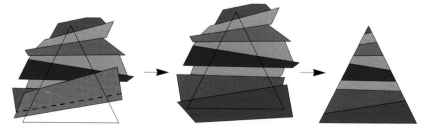

String Piecing Diagram

8. Sew X and X reversed piece to opposite sides of tree triangle, using edge of paper patterns as seam guides.
9. Repeat steps 2–8 to make 46 pine tree tops.

MAKING MAPLE TREES

1. Referring to *Maple Tree Diagram*, draw master pattern on graph paper.

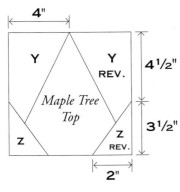

Maple Tree Diagram

2. With shiny side down, lay freezer paper over master pattern and trace pattern onto freezer paper. Cut out freezer-paper patterns for Y, Y reversed, Z, Z reversed, and tree top.
3. Press Y, Y reversed, Z, and Z reversed patterns onto muslin as you did for X pieces. Cut out muslin pieces.
4. String-piece maple tree top.
5. To complete block, sew Y and Y reversed pieces to opposite sides of tree top as shown in diagram; then add Z pieces.
6. Repeat steps 2–5 to make 12 maple tree tops.

FINISHING TREE BLOCKS

1. Remove paper patterns from backs of sewn blocks. (Small scissors or a seam ripper may be helpful.) Be careful not to pull out stitching when removing paper from string-piecing. Press seam allowances toward muslin.
(continued)

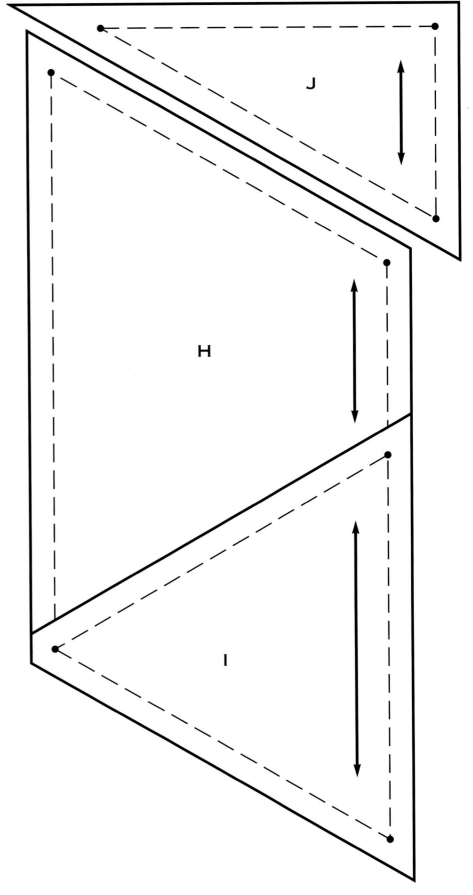

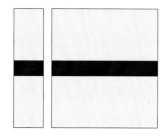

Tree Trunk Strip Set Diagram

2. Referring to *Tree Trunk Strip Set Diagram,* join strips of muslin and dark brown fabric. Make 4 strip sets.
3. From tree trunk strip sets, cut 58 (2½"-wide) segments as shown.
4. Sew a tree trunk section to bottom of each tree top.

QUILT ASSEMBLY

1. Referring to *Quilt Assembly Diagram,* lay out tree and house blocks in 9 horizontal rows. Note that rows 1, 3, 4, and 7 have muslin spacer strips to make rows same length.
2. Join blocks into rows. Press seam allowances in opposite directions from row to row. Join horizontal rows. Press seam allowances.
3. Join matching paisley fabric border strips end-to-end to make 2 side borders and 2 shorter borders for top and bottom.
4. Measure length of quilt through middle of quilt. Trim side borders to this length plus 5½" (finished width of 1 border), approximately 96½". Measure quilt width in same manner and trim top and bottom borders to this measurement plus 5½", approximately 74½".
5. Borders are numbered on *Quilt Assembly Diagram* in order sewn. Border 1 seam is partially stitched and then completed after Border 4 is added. To begin, align end of Border 1 with top left corner of quilt top. With right sides facing, join border to

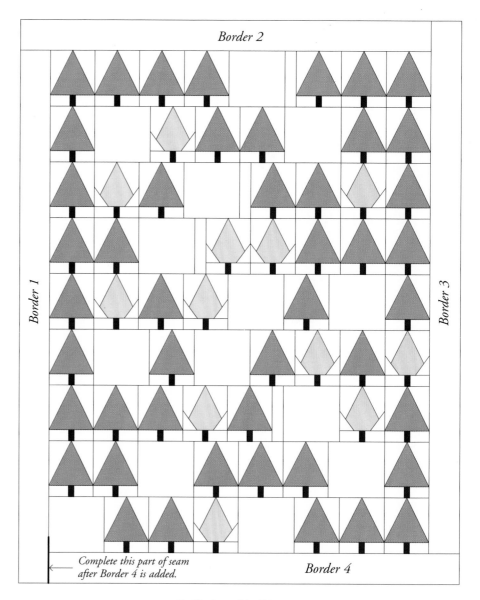

Complete this part of seam after Border 4 is added.

Quilt Assembly Diagram

left edge of quilt, but stop stitching 3" before bottom corner of quilt. (Border will be longer than quilt.) Do not trim excess border strip. Press seam allowance toward border.
6. Sew Border 2 to top edge of quilt, stitching across Border 1. Add borders 3 and 4 in same manner; then complete seam at bottom of Border 1 as shown on *Quilt Assembly Diagram.* Press seam allowances toward borders.

QUILTING AND FINISHING

1. Divide backing fabric into 2 equal lengths. Cut 1 panel in half lengthwise. Sew a narrow panel to each side of wide panel. Layer backing, batting, and quilt top; baste.
2. Quilt as desired. The quilt shown is outline-quilted along row seams and around house and tree shapes.
3. See General Instructions (page 174) for directions on making and applying binding. Make 375" of straight-grain binding.

VALLEY JUNCTION

Marilyn set 20 Wedding Ring blocks together in a way that allowed space for elaborate feather quilting. Setting triangles are extra large so the blocks "float" at the outer edges without touching the inner border. You can use any 10" block in this setting.

Finished size of quilt: 75½" x 89¾"   **Finished size of block:** 10" square

MATERIALS

5 yards of muslin or white fabric
1¾ yards of red print fabric for inner
   border and binding
⅛ yard *each* or scraps of 19 red fabrics
5½ yards of backing fabric or
   2¾ yards of 90"-wide muslin
81" x 96" (full-size) precut batting
Rotary cutter, acrylic ruler, and
   cutting mat
Template plastic (optional)

CUTTING

Refer to block diagram to identify
each piece by letter. For traditional
cutting and piecing, make templates
for patterns A and B on page 63.

From red border fabric, cut:

♥ 8 (2"-wide) strips for binding.
♥ 8 (2½"-wide) border strips.
   Add remainder of border fabric to
   assorted reds for blocks.

From *each* of 20 red fabrics, cut:

♥ 1 (2⅞"-wide) strip.
   From this, cut 8 (2⅞") squares.
   Cut each square in half diagonally
   to get 16 B triangles. From
   remainder, cut 4 (2½") A squares.

From muslin, cut:

♥ 2 (7½" x 96") lengthwise strips for
   side borders.
♥ 2 (7½" x 85") lengthwise strips for
   top and bottom borders.
♥ 3 (2½" x 85") lengthwise strips.
   From these, cut 100 (2½") A
   squares.
♥ 3 (10½"-wide) crosswise strips.
   From these, cut 12 (10½") setting
   squares.
♥ 2 (16¼"-wide) crosswise strips.
   From these, cut 4 (16¼") squares
   and 2 (9½") squares.
   Cut each 16¼" square diagonally
   in *both* directions to get 14 setting
   triangles and 2 extra.
   Cut each 9½" square in half diagonally to get 4 corner triangles.
♥ 8 (2⅞"-wide) crosswise strips.
   From these and remaining scraps,
   cut 160 (2⅞") squares.
   Cut each square in half diagonally
   to get 320 B triangles.

PIECING BLOCKS

1. Referring to *Block Assembly Diagram*, select 4 A squares and 16 B triangles of the same red fabric for 1 block.

2. Join red and muslin B triangles to make 16 triangle-squares. Press seam allowances toward red fabric.

3. Referring to *Block Assembly Diagram*, join red and muslin A squares with triangle-squares to make 5 horizontal rows as shown. Press seam allowances in opposite directions from row to row.

4. Join rows to complete block.

5. Make 20 blocks, 1 from each red fabric. *(continued)*

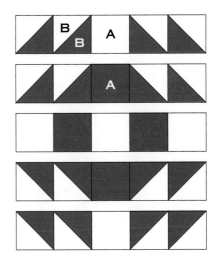

Block Assembly Diagram

*Designed and made by Marilyn Parks of Des Moines, Iowa, with members
of the Des Moines Area Quilters Guild, 1992. Hand-quilted by Ethel Jordan.*

Quilt Assembly

1. Referring to Quilt Assembly Diagram, arrange blocks, setting squares, and setting triangles in diagonal rows. Heavy lines on diagram indicate rows.

2. Join blocks in rows. To add setting triangles, align right angle of triangle with block corner.

3. Join rows.

4. Sew a corner triangle to each corner of quilt top. Press seam allowances toward triangles.

5. Join 2 red border strips end-to-end to make 1 border. Make 4 borders.

6. Fold each muslin border strip in half and mark center. Aligning center of each muslin border with center seam of 1 red strip, join strips to make 4 double borders. Press seam allowances toward red strips.

7. See General Instructions (page 169) for tips on mitered border corners. Join borders to quilt top. Press seam allowances toward borders; then stitch corner seams.

Quilting and Finishing

1. Divide backing fabric into 2 (2¾-yard) lengths. Cut 1 panel in half lengthwise. Sew a narrow panel to each side of wide panel. Press seam allowances toward narrow panels.

2. Mark quilting designs on quilt top. Marilyn customized her own feather motifs for the setting pieces and borders. Draft your own designs or use ready-made stencils to mark quilting designs as desired.

3. Layer backing, batting, and quilt top; baste. Quilt as desired.

4. See General Instructions (page 174) for directions on making and applying binding. Make 345" of straight-grain binding.

Quilt Assembly Diagram

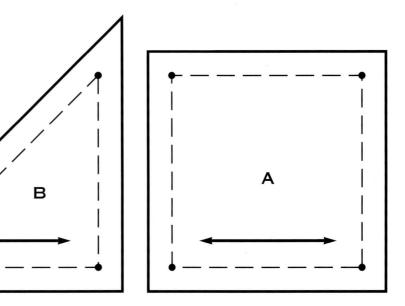

Organizing a Cutting Bee

A fabric cutting bee is a fun way to add to the variety of fabrics for scrap quilts. And what better way to spend a day than with four or five quilting friends, augmenting the cutting with lots of talk and a good supply of chocolate. Everyone catches up on what's happening and goes home with enough cut strips to start sewing.

Choose a Color Scheme

We begin a cutting bee by choosing a mood or color scheme for our quilts. For example, we could decide that our quilts will use only pastel fabrics. Or we could opt for old-fashioned plaids, checks, and stripes mixed with cream prints.

On the day of the bee, each person brings 10 yards of assorted fabrics that fit the color scheme, selecting a balance of light, medium, and dark values. We also bring rotary cutting supplies, plastic sweater boxes to carry cut strips, irons and ironing boards, and food for a potluck lunch.

Cutting Strips

Our bees are usually "twosey-foursey" cutting sessions. That is, we cut strips that will give us 2" and 4" *finished size* squares and triangles.

When we use regular cutting tools, we cut strips 2⅞" wide and 4⅞" wide. But if we will be using triangle rulers, designed for cutting right triangles from strips, then we cut strips 2½" wide and 4½" wide instead. (See page 69 for instructions on how to use these specialized rulers.)

Trade for Variety

From each fabric, we cut one wide strip and one narrow strip for *each* participant.

We cut until our sweater boxes are full or until our wrists give out, whichever comes first. (All this cutting is, of course, punctuated with lively conversation.) When we've cut all the fabric we brought, then everyone trades strips. After the exchange, everyone has strips of the fabric she brought, *plus* strips of everyone else's fabric—an enhanced variety of strips in both widths.

Pieces into Blocks

If time allows, each person cuts the strips into the pieces she needs for her quilt. To use the strips efficiently, we choose blocks with basic patchwork shapes: A triangles that finish with 2" legs, B triangles that finish with 4" legs, C squares that finish 2", and D squares that finish 4".

In addition to Liz's Star block and the Corn and Beans block, the blocks shown here work well with twosey-foursey pieces.

BRAVE NEW WORLD BLOCK

WORLD'S FAIR BLOCK

CAT'S CRADLE BLOCK

ROCKY ROAD BLOCK

LIZ'S SUPER STAR

Liz used strips of antique-looking fabrics from a cutting bee to make 32 star blocks for this quilt. Alternating blocks create the illusion of stars within stars. Liz used the diagonal-corner method to make the Goose Chase units for the pieced border.

Finished size of quilt: 76" x 92"   **Finished size of block:** 8" square

MATERIALS

Fabrics listed indicate numbers and widths of cutting-bee strips needed to make a quilt like the one shown.

32 (2⅞" x 42") strips and 20
   (4⅞" x 21") strips of assorted
   medium and dark fabrics*
52 (2⅞" x 42") strips and 28
   (4⅞" x 21") strips of assorted
   light fabrics*
8 (2½" x 42") strips of assorted blue
   fabrics for inner border
¾ yard of binding fabric
6 yards of backing fabric or 3 yards of
   90"-wide muslin
81" x 96" (full-size) precut batting
Triangle ruler or template plastic
Note: To use a triangle ruler to
quick-cut A and B triangles from
strips, start with 2½"-wide and 4½"-
wide strips rather than strip widths
stated. See tip box on page 69 to
learn how to use a triangle ruler to
cut right triangles from a strip.

CUTTING

Before cutting pieces, read instructions carefully and choose quick piecing or traditional methods for the construction of each unit. For traditional cutting and piecing methods, make templates for patterns A, B, C, D, and X on page 68. Refer to diagrams to identify each piece by letter.

From *each* 2⅞"-wide medium/dark strip, cut:
❤ 4 (2⅞") squares.
   Cut each square in half diagonally
   to get 8 A triangles for small stars.
❤ 5 (2½" x 4½") rectangles *or* 5 X
   triangles for Goose Chase units.

From *each* 4⅞"-wide medium/dark strip, cut:
❤ 4 (4⅞") squares.
   Cut each square in half diagonally
   to get 8 B triangles for large stars.

From *each* of 32 (2⅞"-wide) light strips, cut:
❤ 4 (2⅞") squares.
   Cut each square in half diagonally
   to get 8 A triangles for small stars.
❤ 8 (2½") C squares.

From *each* of 20 (2⅞"-wide) light strips, cut:
❤ 16 (2½") squares *or* 16 A triangles
   for Goose Chase units.

From *each* of 20 (4⅞"-wide) light strips, cut:
❤ 4 (4⅞") squares.
   Cut each square in half diagonally
   to get 8 B triangles for large stars.

From 8 (4⅞"-wide) light strips, cut:
❤ 32 (4½") D squares.

MAKING STAR BLOCKS

1. Select 8 A triangles of 1 dark fabric. Referring to *Block Assembly Diagram,* join each of these with an A triangle of a different light fabric to make 8 triangle-squares.

2. Arrange triangle-squares and 8 C squares in 4 horizontal rows as shown. Join units in rows. Press seam allowances in alternate directions from row to row. Join rows.

3. Repeat to make 32 star blocks.

(continued)

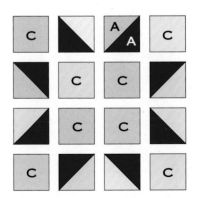

Block Assembly Diagram

Designed and made by Liz Porter, 1994. Machine-quilted by Fern Stewart.

MAKING B UNITS

1. Select 8 B triangles of 1 dark fabric. Join each of these with a B triangle of a different light fabric to make 8 triangle-squares. Press seam allowances toward darker fabric.

2. Referring to *B Unit Diagram,* join 2 triangle-squares as shown.

3. Make 4 B units for each of 20 large stars.

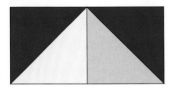

B Unit Diagram

JOINING BLOCKS

Note: Press seam allowances toward B units throughout.

1. Referring to Row 1 of *Row Assembly Diagram,* join 4 B units and 8 D squares in a horizontal row for top of quilt.

2. Referring to Row 2 of *Row Assembly Diagram,* position a star block below each B unit of Row A. Fill in spaces at sides and between blocks with B units, coordinating B unit fabrics with those in Row 1 as shown. Join blocks in Row 2.

3. Referring to Row 3 of *Row Assembly Diagram,* position a matching B unit below each star block in Row 2. Join these with contrasting B units as shown. Then fill in spaces between B units with star blocks. Add a pair of D squares to both ends to complete Row 3 as shown.

4. Continue making rows 2 and 3 in sequence, carefully selecting B units to correspond with previous row. End sequence with fifth Row 2.

5. Referring to quilt photograph, join remaining B units and D squares to make 1 more of Row 1 for bottom of quilt, turning B units upside down to correspond with previous row.

6. Join rows.

ADDING INNER BORDER

1. Cut blue inner border strips into random lengths, 4"–27" long.

2. For side borders, join assorted strips to make 2 (80½"-long) borders. Sew borders to sides of quilt. Press

seam allowances toward borders.

3. For top and bottom borders, join remaining strips to make 2 (68½"-long) borders. Sew borders to top and bottom quilt edges. Press seam allowances toward borders.

MAKING GOOSE CHASE UNITS

1. See General Instructions (page 165) for directions on diagonal-corner method. Following those instructions, join 2 (2½") light squares to corners of 1 (2½" x 4½") rectangle to make 1 Goose Chase unit. To make Goose Chase units traditionally, join a light A triangle to each side of X triangle to make 1 Goose Chase unit as shown in *Traditional Goose Chase Unit Diagram.*

2. Using chosen piecing method, make 160 Goose Chase units. Press seam allowances toward light triangles.

(continued)

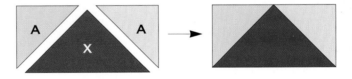

Traditional Goose Chase Unit Diagram

Row Assembly Diagram

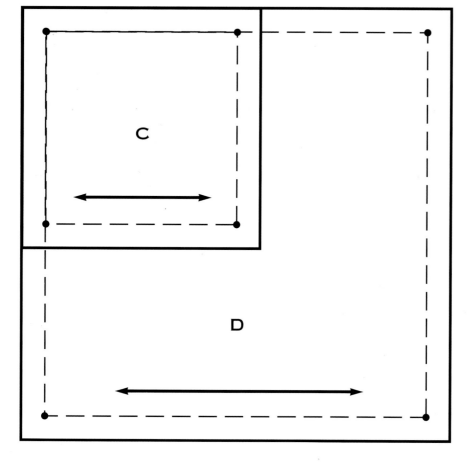

ADDING GOOSE CHASE BORDER

1. Join 36 Goose Chase units for each top and bottom border. Join 44 units for each side border.

2. Top border seam is partially stitched and then completed after fourth border is added. With right sides facing, pin top border in place, aligning it with top right corner of quilt. (Border will be longer than quilt top). Starting at top right corner, stitch border to quilt top, leaving last 5 Goose Chase units unsewn at left corner. Press seam allowances toward inner border.

3. Sew 1 side border to right side of quilt. Then add bottom border to bottom edge and last side border to left side. Press seam allowances toward inner border.

4. Complete seam on top border, stitching 5 Goose Chase units to top left corner of quilt top and across top of left side border.

USING SPECIAL RULERS TO CUT TRIANGLES FROM STRIPS

With most cutting tools, you need strips of different sizes to cut squares and triangles, even if the legs of the squares and right triangles eventually have the same *finished* size. The extra fabric at the triangle tips creates the discrepancy in cut size. Since those tips get trimmed from the seam allowance in the end, it makes sense to eliminate this extra fabric from the start so you can cut both shapes from one strip.

Triangle rulers, designed for cutting right triangles with legs on the straight-of-grain, let you cut triangles and squares of the same finished size from one strip. These rulers are available in several sizes and configurations. For this application, choose a ruler that measures the length of the triangle leg.

You can use any standard ruler to cut a square. The steps below illustrate how to use a triangle ruler to cut right triangles from the same strip.

Cut a strip ½" wider than desired *finished* size of squares or triangle legs. For our example, we cut a 2½"-wide strip. Square-off left end of strip.

1. To prepare to cut triangles, align bottom of ruler with bottom of strip. Slide ruler to the left until markings on ruler are aligned for the size you want to cut (2½" in our example).

2. Cut along slanted edge of ruler. Top tip of cut triangle will be blunt because there is no excess fabric beyond the seam allowance.

3. To cut next triangle, reposition ruler as shown, aligning diagonal edge of ruler with cut edge of fabric. Cut along straight side of ruler.

Continue alternating position of ruler to cut additional triangles.

QUILTING AND FINISHING

1. Divide backing fabric into 2 (3-yard) lengths. Cut 1 piece in half lengthwise. Sew a narrow panel to each side of wide piece. Press seam allowances toward narrow panels.

2. Mark desired quilting designs on quilt top. Quilt shown has a small cable quilted in inner border and diagonal lines, spaced 2" apart, quilted through blocks.

3. Layer backing, batting, and quilt top; baste. Quilt as desired.

4. See General Instructions (page 174) for directions on making and applying binding. Make 350" of straight-grain binding.

CORN AND BEANS

This quilt got its start at a group cutting bee that yielded a variety of fabrics for each of 24 blocks. See the tip box on page 64 on how to organize your own bee and for ideas of other blocks to make from cutting-bee strips.

Finished size of quilt: 62" x 86"　　**Finished size of block:** 12" square

MATERIALS

Fabrics listed indicate numbers and widths of cutting-bee strips needed to make a quilt similar to the one shown.

36 (2⅞" x 21") strips and 12 (4⅞" x 21") strips of assorted medium and dark fabrics*

36 (2⅞" x 21") and 12 (4⅞" x 21") strips of assorted light fabrics*

1½ yards of brown print fabric for outer border

⅔ yard of red fabric for inner border

¾ yard of binding fabric

5¼ yards of backing fabric or 2¾ yards of 90"-wide muslin

81" x 96" (full-size) precut batting

Triangle ruler or template plastic

*Note: To use a triangle ruler to quick-cut A and B triangles from strips, start with 2½"-wide and 4½"-wide strips rather than strip widths stated. See tip box on page 69 to learn how to use a triangle ruler to cut right triangles from a strip.

CUTTING

Refer to diagrams to identify each piece by letter. For traditional cutting and piecing methods, make templates for patterns A and B on page 68.

From all 2⅞"-wide strips, cut:

❤ 240 (2⅞") light squares and 240 (2⅞") medium/dark squares. Cut each square in half diagonally to get 960 A triangles.

From all 4⅞"-wide strips, cut:

❤ 48 (4⅞") light squares and 48 (4⅞") medium/dark squares. Cut each square in half diagonally to get 192 B triangles.

From brown print fabric, cut:

❤ 8 (5½" x 42") outer border strips.

From red fabric, cut:

❤ 8 (2½" x 42") inner border strips.

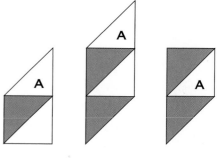

Unit X　　*Unit Y*　　*Unit Z*

PIECING BLOCKS

1. Join pairs of dark and light A triangles to make 288 triangle-squares.

2. Referring to *unit diagrams,* join triangle-squares with single triangles to make 96 *each* of units X, Y, and Z. Press seam allowances away from triangle-squares in each unit.

3. Referring to *Quarter-Block Assembly Diagram,* join units as shown. Add B triangles (1 dark and 1 light) as shown to complete quarter-block. Make 96 quarter-blocks.

(continued)

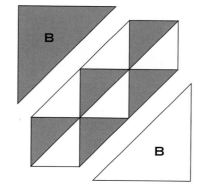
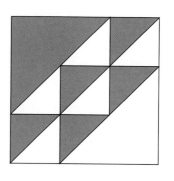

Quarter-Block Assembly Diagram

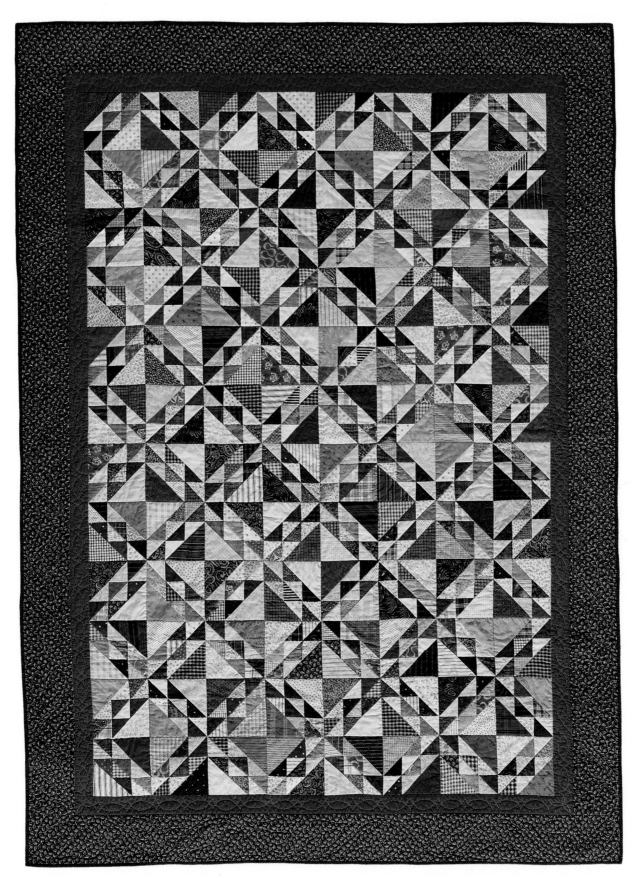

Designed and made by Marianne Fons, 1994. Machine-quilted by Fern Stewart.

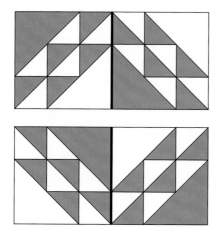

Block Assembly Diagram

4. Referring to *Block Assembly Diagram,* join 4 quarter-blocks in 2 rows of 2 blocks per row, positioning light and dark B triangles as shown. Press seam allowances in opposite directions from row to row.

5. Join rows to make 1 Corn and Beans block. Make 24 blocks.

QUILT ASSEMBLY

1. Referring to *Row Assembly Diagram,* join 4 blocks in a horizontal row. Make 6 rows. Press seam allowances in opposite directions from row to row.

2. Referring to photograph on page 71, join rows.

3. For inner borders, join 2 red border strips end-to-end to make each border. Make 4 borders. For outer borders, assemble 4 borders from brown border strips in same manner.

4. Measure length of quilt top, measuring through middle rather than along sides. Trim 2 inner borders to this length (approximately 72½"). Sew these to quilt sides, easing as necessary. Press seam allowances toward borders.

5. Measure quilt width, including side borders. Trim remaining inner borders to this length (approximately 52½"). Join these to top and bottom edges of quilt. Press seam allowances toward borders.

6. In same manner, add outer borders to sides and ends of quilt top.

QUILTING AND FINISHING

1. Divide backing fabric into 2 equal lengths. Cut 1 piece in half lengthwise into 2 narrow panels. Join a narrow panel to each side of wide piece. Press seams toward narrow panels.

2. Layer backing, batting, and quilt top; baste.

3. Quilt as desired. Quilt shown was outline-quilted by machine.

4. See General Instructions (page 174) for directions on making and applying binding. Make 320" of straight-grain binding.

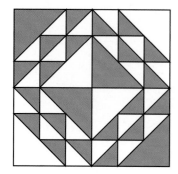
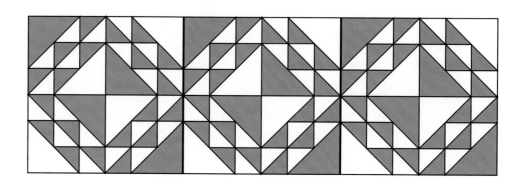

Row Assembly Diagram

WITH A LITTLE HELP FROM MY FRIENDS

Carol Hopkins combined 72 sampler blocks with a nine-patch variation setting block that creates a diagonal chain effect. Cutting and piecing instructions for setting blocks are given for strip piecing only.

Finished size of quilt: 54" x 63"   **Finished size of blocks:** 3" square

MATERIALS

4 yards of ivory fabric
1½" x 21" *each* of 8 assorted fabrics
1" x 42" *each* of 24 assorted fabrics
Scraps of assorted fabrics for blocks
½ yard of binding fabric
4 yards of backing fabric
72" x 90" (twin-size) precut batting
Rotary cutter, acrylic ruler, and
    cutting mat

CUTTING

Cut strips for setting blocks and borders. Refer to diagrams to identify each piece by letter. To cut pieces for sampler blocks, see instructions given for Bonus 3" Blocks section (page 78).

From ivory fabric, cut:
- ♥ 7 (3½"-wide) border strips.
- ♥ 24 (1"-wide) strips for A strip sets.
- ♥ 16 (1½" x 21") strips for B strip sets.

- ♥ 6 (1½"-wide) strips. From these, cut 168 (1½") B squares.
- ♥ 27 (1½"-wide) strips. From these, cut 314 (1½" x 3½") C sashing pieces.
- ♥ 4 (2½"-wide) strips. From these, cut 4 (2½" x 3½") D rectangles and 22 (2½" x 5½") E rectangles.

SAMPLER BLOCKS

Use patterns in the Bonus 3" Blocks section and add additional designs as needed to make 72 blocks.

QUICK PIECING FOUR-PATCH UNITS

1. Referring to *Strip Set A Diagram*, join 1"-wide ivory and colored strips.
2. From these strip sets, cut 1,008 (1"-wide) segments.
3. Referring to *Four-Patch Diagram*, make 504 four-patch units.

Strip Set A Diagram—Make 24.

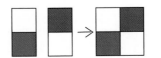

Four-Patch Diagram—Make 504.

QUICK PIECING SETTING BLOCKS

1. Referring to *Strip Set B Diagram*, join 1½" x 21" ivory and colored strips. From these strip sets, cut 97 (1½"-wide) segments.

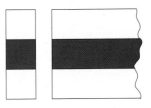

Strip Set B Diagram—Make 8.

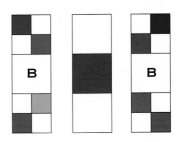

Setting Block Diagram—Make 71.

2. Referring to *Setting Block Diagram*, select 4 four-patch units, 2 ivory B squares, and 1 Strip Set B segment for each block. Join pieces to make 3 vertical rows. Press seam allowances toward B squares.
3. Join rows to complete block. Make 71 setting blocks.

(continued)

Designed and made by Carol Hopkins of West Lafayette, Indiana, with her friends Jackie Conaway, Connie Culverhouse, Cheryl Erskine, Linda Koenig, and Garnet Roesel, 1991.

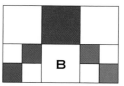

Partial Setting Block Diagram—Make 26.

4. Referring to *Partial Setting Block Diagram*, select 2 four-patch units, 1 ivory B square, and 1 Strip Set B segment for each partial setting block. Join pieces as shown. Make 26 partial setting blocks.

PIECING SASHING UNITS

Referring to *Sashing Unit Diagram*, join 12 four-patch units and 11 C pieces to make a row. Make 14 sashing units.

PIECING BLOCK ROWS

1. Referring to *Row I Assembly Diagram*, join 6 partial setting blocks and 5 E rectangles in a row. Add a C piece to each end of row. (Trim C pieces to match height of partial setting block.) Join a sashing unit to bottom of row as shown. Sew a D rectangle to each end of Row I. Make 2 of Row I.

2. Referring to *Row II Assembly Diagram*, join 5 setting blocks, 2 partial

Sashing Unit Diagram—Make 14.

Row I Assembly Diagram—Make 2.

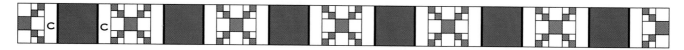

Row II Assembly Diagram—Make 7.

setting blocks, 12 C pieces, and 6 sampler blocks in a row. Make 7 of Row II.

3. Referring to *Row III Assembly Diagram,* join 6 setting blocks, 12 C pieces, and 5 sampler blocks in a row. Add a sashing unit to both long sides of row as shown. Add an E rectangle to each end of Row III. Make 6 of Row III.

QUILT ASSEMBLY

1. Referring to *Quilt Assembly Diagram,* join 7 rows in order shown to assemble half of quilt. Repeat to assemble second half. Referring to

photograph, turn second half upside down and join to first half with remaining Row II between halves.

2. For top and bottom borders, cut 1 border strip into 2 (21"-long) pieces. Join 1½ border strips for each border.

3. Measure width of quilt top through middle of quilt. Trim borders to this length (approximately 49½"). Sew borders to top and bottom edges of quilt.

4. Join 2 border strips for each side border. Measure length of quilt through middle of quilt. Trim side borders to this length (approximately 63½"). Sew borders to quilt sides.

QUILTING AND FINISHING

1. Divide backing fabric into 2 (2-yard) lengths. Cut 1 piece in half lengthwise. Discard 1 narrow piece. Sew remaining narrow panel to 1 side of wide panel. Press seam allowances toward narrow panel.

2. Mark desired quilting designs on quilt top. The quilt shown is outline-quilted and has small swags quilted around sampler blocks and on border.

3. Layer backing, batting, and quilt top; baste. Quilt as desired.

4. See General Instructions (page 174) for directions on making and applying binding. Make 250" of straight-grain binding.

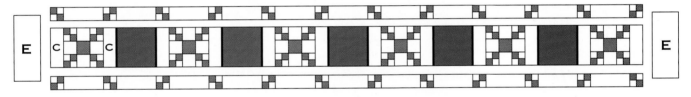

Row III Assembly Diagram—Make 6.

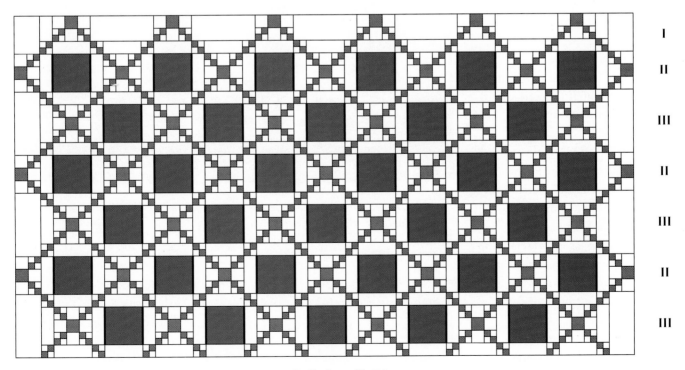

Quilt Assembly Diagram

FRIENDS TO FRIENDS

Connie Culverhouse squared-off 72 blocks with triangles and then set the blocks on point, alternating them with setting squares. For extra interest, she used two colors of setting squares, putting all the blue squares at the quilt's center for a medallion effect.

Finished size of quilt: 64" x 70" **Finished size of blocks:** 3" square

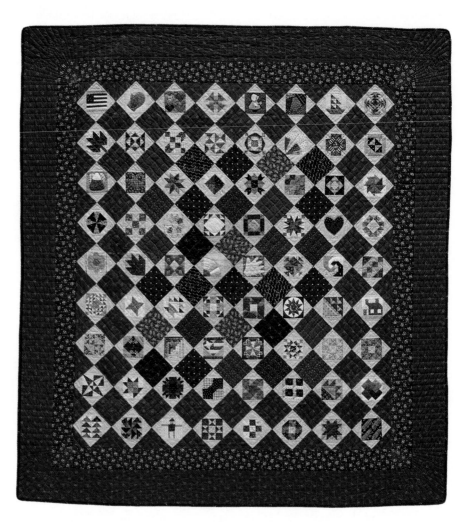

Designed and made by Connie Culverhouse of Lafayette, Indiana, with her friends Jackie Conaway, Cheryl Erskine, Carol Hopkins, Linda Koenig, and Garnet Roesel, 1991.

MATERIALS

2¾ yards of burgundy fabric
1½ yards of cream print fabric
1 yard of blue fabric for inner border
¼ yard *each* or scraps of 6 blue fabrics
    for setting squares
Scraps of assorted fabrics for blocks
½ yard of navy fabric for binding
4 yards of backing fabric
72" x 90" (twin-size) precut batting
Template plastic and/or plastic-coated
    freezer paper (optional)

CUTTING

Follow instructions below to cut setting pieces, borders, and X triangles. For traditional cutting, make a template for pattern X on page 77.

Add remaining fabrics to scraps for sampler blocks. To cut pieces for sampler blocks, see instructions given for Bonus 3" Blocks section (page 78).

From burgundy fabric, cut:
♥ 8 (5½"-wide) strips for outer
    border.

♥ 4 (4¾"-wide) strips.
    From these, cut 26 (4¾") setting
    squares.
♥ 2 (3⅞") squares.
    Cut each square in half diagonally
    to get 4 corner triangles.

♥ 2 (7¼"-wide) strips.
    From these, cut 8 (7¼") squares.
    Cut each square in half diagonally
    in *both* directions to get 30 setting
    triangles and 2 extra.

76

From cream print fabric, cut:
- ❤ 11 (3"-wide) strips.
  From these, cut 144 (3") squares. Cut each square in half diagonally to get 288 X triangles.

From blue border fabric, cut:
- ❤ 7 (3½"-wide) strips.

From assorted blue fabrics, cut:
- ❤ 30 (4¾") setting squares.

MAKING SAMPLER BLOCKS

Use patterns in the Bonus 3" Blocks section and add additional designs as needed to make 72 blocks.

SQUARING-OFF BLOCKS

Adding triangle corners to each sampler block is necessary to set the blocks on point. Join cream X triangles to sides of each block, beginning with opposite sides and then completing remaining sides.

QUILT ASSEMBLY

1. Referring to *Quilt Assembly Diagram*, lay out blocks, setting squares, setting triangles, and corner triangles in diagonal rows. Heavy lines on diagram indicate rows. Join blocks and setting pieces in rows.

2. Join rows.

3. For inner borders, join 2 blue strips for each side border. Cut 1 remaining strip in half. Join 1½ strips each for top and bottom borders.

4. For outer borders, join 2 red strips for each border.

5. Matching centers, sew 1 inner border to each outer border.

6. See General Instructions (page 169) for directions on mitered border corners. Join borders to quilt top. Press seam allowances toward borders; then stitch corner seams.

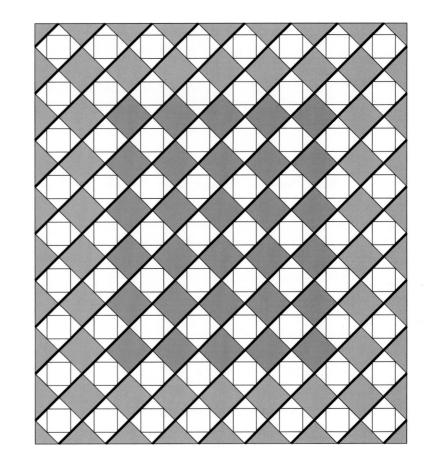

Quilt Assembly Diagram

QUILTING AND FINISHING

1. Divide backing fabric into 2 (2-yard) lengths. Cut 1 piece in half lengthwise. Sew a narrow panel to each side of wide panel.

2. Mark desired quilting designs on quilt top. The quilt shown is outline-quilted, with 1" cross-hatching quilted in setting squares. Perpendicular lines are quilted through borders, converging into a fan at each corner.

3. Layer backing, batting, and quilt top; baste. (Backing seams will parallel top and bottom quilt edges.) Quilt as desired.

4. See General Instructions (page 174) for directions on making and applying binding. Make 285" of straight-grain binding.

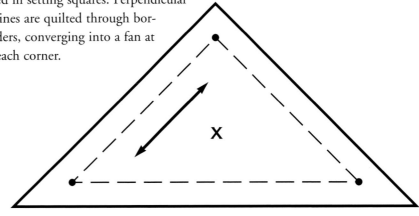

BONUS 3" BLOCKS

Choose from this collection of mini-blocks when making *Friends to Friends* (page 52), *With a Little Help from My Friends* (page 53), *Chatelaine & Sewing Kit* (page 12), or *Advent Calendar* (page 127).

This section includes *finished-size* drawings of 44 blocks. Space does not permit us to offer all 72 blocks used in the sampler quilts. However, many of those blocks are quite simple, and it should be easy for you to draft your own 3"-square block patterns on graph paper.

For patchwork, make templates or rotary-cut each piece, adding ¼" seam allowances on all edges.

For appliqué, make templates for each piece. Appliqué pieces in alphabetical order onto 3½" background squares. If your project won't be subjected to extensive wear, you can use paper-backed fusible webbing to fuse the pieces to the background.

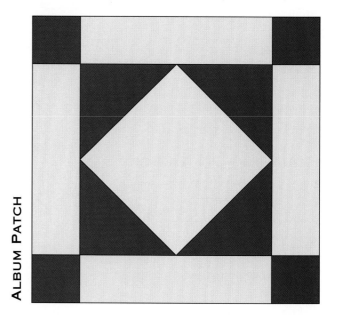

ALBUM PATCH

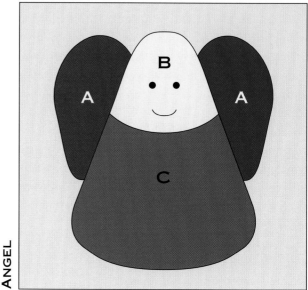

ANGEL

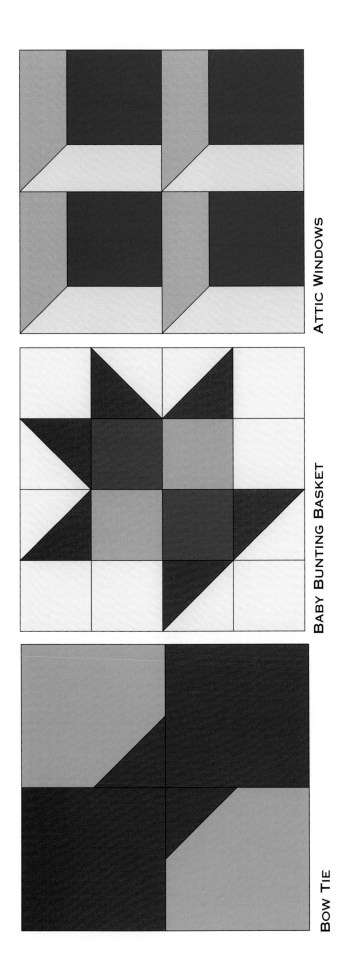

ATTIC WINDOWS

BABY BUNTING BASKET

BOW TIE

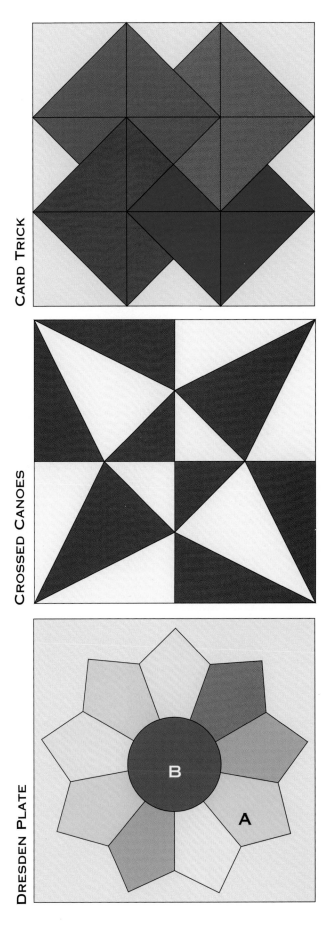

CARD TRICK

CROSSED CANOES

DRESDEN PLATE

79

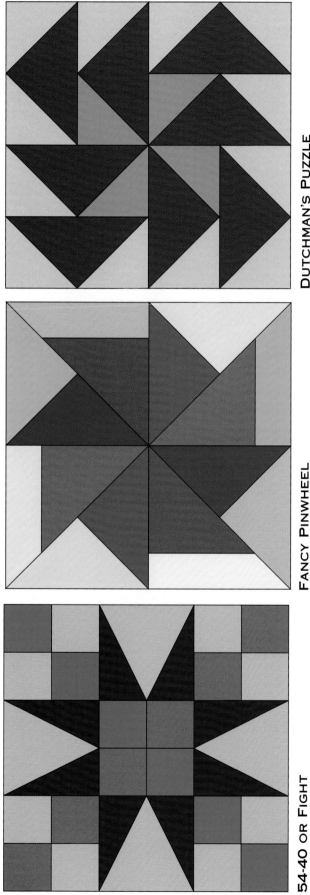

54-40 OR FIGHT

DUTCHMAN'S PUZZLE

FANCY PINWHEEL

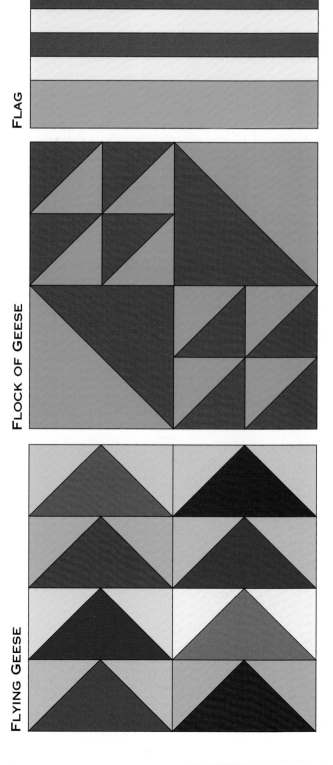

FLAG

FLOCK OF GEESE

FLYING GEESE

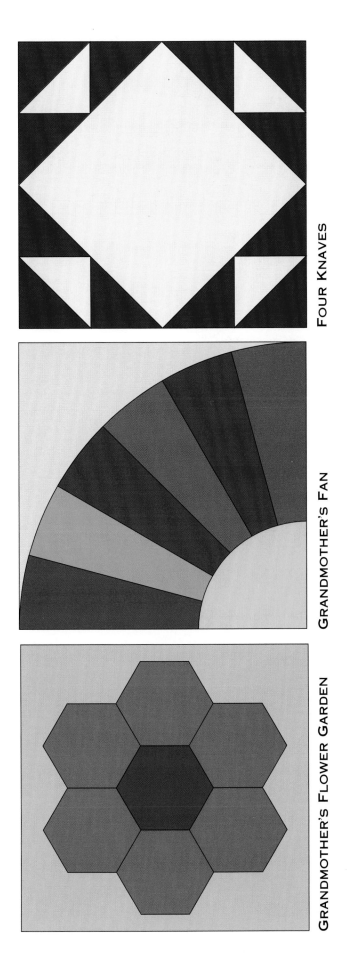

FOUR KNAVES

GRANDMOTHER'S FAN

GRANDMOTHER'S FLOWER GARDEN

HEART

HOURGLASS

KITTY

Lancaster Rose

Maple Leaf

Lonely Lily

Maud's Album Block

Magic Circle

Melon Patch

82

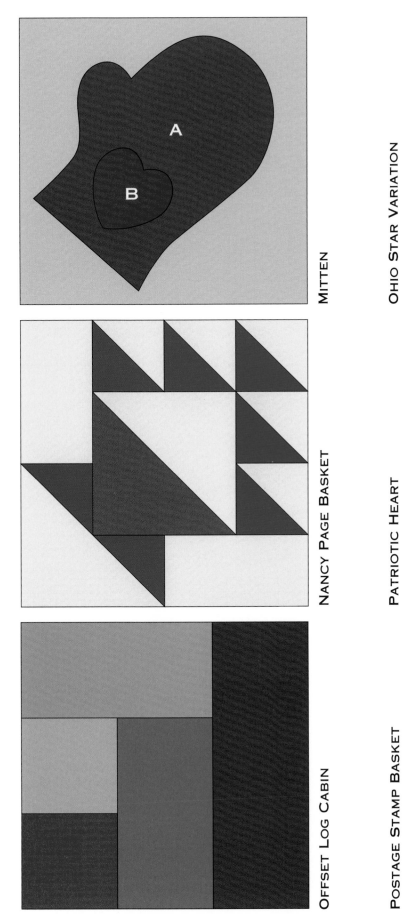

MITTEN

NANCY PAGE BASKET

OFFSET LOG CABIN

OHIO STAR VARIATION

PATRIOTIC HEART

POSTAGE STAMP BASKET

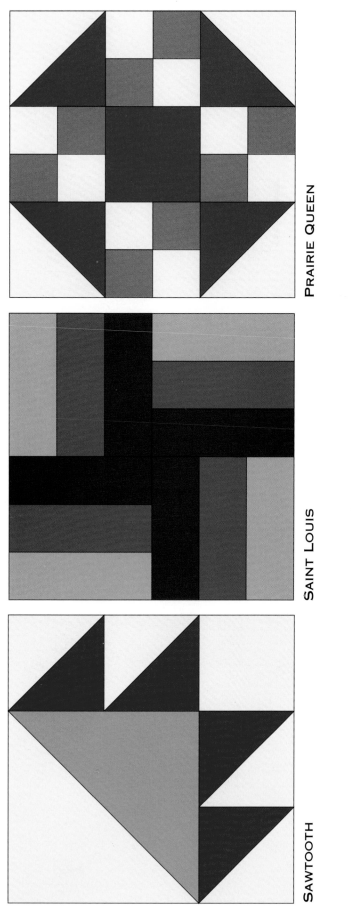

PRAIRIE QUEEN

SAINT LOUIS

SAWTOOTH

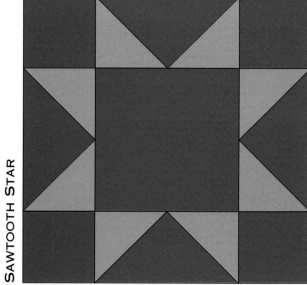

SAWTOOTH STAR

SCHOOLHOUSE

SPOOL

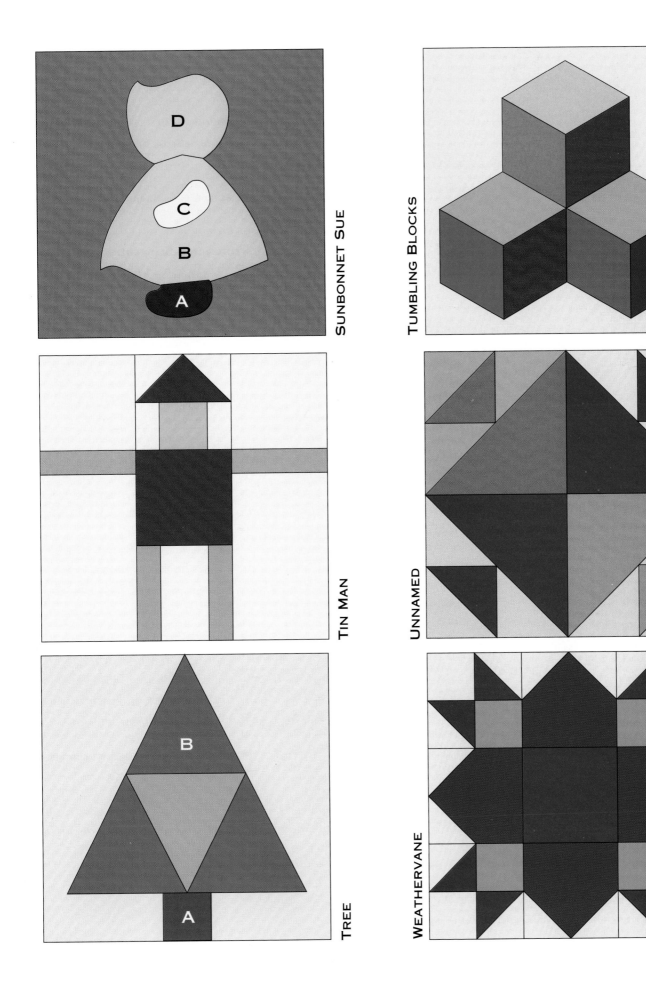

SUNBONNET SUE

TUMBLING BLOCKS

TIN MAN

UNNAMED

TREE

WEATHERVANE

85

STRING STAR

*For the star block, Liz used freezer-paper templates to cut diamonds from
strip-pieced patchwork. Then she passed the block on to three friends who added decorative borders.
The appliqué is done by machine, but it can also be buttonhole-stitched by hand.*

Finished size of quilt: 52" x 52"   **Finished size of center star:** 18¾" square

MATERIALS

1⅝ yards of tan fabric for outer border
1 yard of green fabric for vine and
  leaves
1 yard of red print fabric for star,
  middle border strips, and binding
½ yard of cream fabric for inner border
¼ yard of dark beige fabric for
  middle border
Assorted fabric scraps for patchwork
  and appliqué
3¼ yards of backing fabric
72" x 90" (twin-size) quilt batting
1½ yards of paper-backed fusible
  webbing (optional)
Hand-sewing needle and brassy-gold
  pearl cotton for hand appliqué
Rotary cutter, acrylic ruler, and
  cutting mat
⅜"-wide bias bar
Tracing paper and freezer paper
Template plastic
Note: Fabric amounts listed are guidelines to make a quilt like the one
shown. Liz's friends enjoyed adding
compatible scraps to her basic fabrics.

CUTTING

To fuse appliqué pieces, trace patterns
the required number of times onto
paper side of fusible web. Rough-cut
shapes and fuse to wrong sides of
appropriate fabrics. For traditional
appliqué, omit fusing and pin appliqués in place. *Note:* Fabric pieces will
be reversed from appliqué patterns.
To cut reversed birds, first trace bird
pattern onto tracing paper. Darken
image on wrong side of paper and use
reversed drawing to make paper templates for half of birds.

For traditional cutting, piecing,
and appliqué methods, make templates for appliqué and patchwork
patterns on pages 90-91. Refer to diagrams to identify pieces by letter.

Even if you are rotary cutting, you
will need a template for diamond A.

From green fabric, cut:

❤ 1 (18") square.
  From this, cut 1⅛"-wide *bias*
  strips. Piece strips as necessary to
  get 8 (22"-long) strips for vines.
❤ 40 leaves.

From red print fabric, cut:

❤ 2 (1½" x 36½") strips and 2 (1½"
  x 38½") strips for middle border.
❤ 6 (2"-wide) strips for binding.
❤ 1 (9") square.
  Cut square in half diagonally in
  both directions to get 4 B triangles.
❤ 4 (6") C squares.

From tan fabric, cut:

❤ 4 (7½" x 56") lengthwise strips for
  outer border.

From cream fabric, cut:

❤ 4 (3⅝"-wide) strips for inner
  border.

From dark beige fabric, cut:

❤ 2 (1½" x 28½") and 2 (1½" x
  30½") for middle border.

From assorted scraps, cut:

❤ 15 strips, each 42" long, cut
  ¾"–2" wide for string patchwork.
❤ 20 (3⅞") squares from
  medium/dark fabrics and 2 (3⅞")
  squares from light fabrics. Cut
  each square in half diagonally to
  get 44 D triangles.
❤ 20 (4¼") squares from light fabrics and 2 (4¼") squares from
  medium/dark fabrics. Cut each
  square in half diagonally in *both*
  directions to get 88 E triangles.
❤ 4 birds and 4 reversed birds.
❤ 8 bird wings.
❤ 8 star flowers and 8 flower centers.
❤ 8 tulips and 8 tulip tips.
❤ 4 baskets and 4 hearts.
❤ 32 cherries.

(continued)

Designed and made by Liz Porter and friends, the May Group, 1994.

Diamond Cutting Diagram

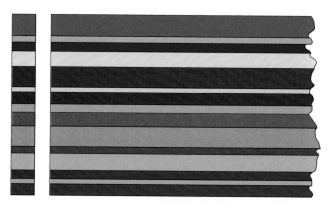

Strip Set Cutting Diagram

MAKING CENTER STAR

1. Use template to draw 8 A diamonds on paper (non-shiny) side of freezer paper. Cut out paper diamonds. These templates do not include seam allowances; you will add seam allowances when cutting fabric.

2. Join assorted strips to make a strip set that is approximately 17" x 42", assembling them in a pleasing arrangement of colors and strip widths.

3. Using a dry iron set at wool, press shiny side of freezer-paper templates to wrong side of strip set as shown in *Diamond Cutting Diagram.* Leave space around paper diamonds for ¼" seam allowances on all sides.

4. Use a rotary cutter and ruler to cut diamonds. Align edge of ruler ¼" beyond edges of paper pieces. Cut out 8 diamonds, adding ¼" seam allowances to all sides as shown. Leave paper adhered to fabric. Save remainder of strip set for borders.

5. Before piecing star, see tip box (page 29) on Setting In Patchwork Pieces. Using paper edges as sewing guides, join diamonds in pairs as shown in *Diagram 1.* Backstitch at beginning and end of seams and stitch only the length of paper pieces, leaving seam allowances free at ends of seams. Join pairs into 4-diamond half stars.

6. Join star halves, again leaving seam allowances at ends of seams free. Press seam allowances to 1 side in a clockwise direction.

7. Referring to *Diagram 2,* set a B triangle into alternate openings around star.

8. Referring to *Diagram 3,* set a C square into each remaining opening. Completed block should measure 19¼", including seam allowances. If your block is larger or smaller, adjust inner border to achieve recommended overall size.

ADDING INNER BORDER

1. Referring to *Strip Set Cutting Diagram,* cut 14 (1¼"-wide) segments from strip set left over from cutting diamonds.

2. Join segments end-to-end to make a continuous strip approximately 230" long.

3. From long strip, cut 2 borders 19¼" long and 2 borders 20¾" long. Sew shorter borders to opposite sides of star; sew longer borders to remaining sides. Press seam allowances toward borders. (All borders, except mitered outer borders, will be added to quilt top in this manner.)

4. Trim 2 cream border strips to 20¾" long and 2 strips to 27" long. Sew borders to center square.

5. From remainder of pieced strip, cut 2 borders 27" long and 2 borders 28½" long. Sew borders to cream border as before. Quilt top should now measure approximately 28½".

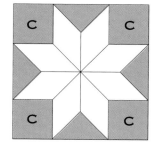

Diagram 1

Diagram 2

Diagram 3

ADDING MIDDLE BORDER

1. Sew dark beige border strips to quilt. Press seam allowances toward beige borders.

2. Referring to *Middle Border Unit Diagram,* join 2 light E triangles to make a larger triangle. Sew this triangle to a medium/dark D triangle to make a square. Make 40 border units.

3. Referring to *Middle Border Corner Unit Diagram,* make 4 border corner units in same manner, joining 2 dark E triangles and 1 light D triangle to make each unit.

4. Referring to *Border Diagram,* join 10 border units in a row to make each border. Each row is assembled in same manner, with dark D triangles always in upper left corner of unit.

5. Referring to *Border Diagram,* sew 2 pieced borders to opposite sides of quilt top. Join corner units to ends of remaining borders; then add these borders to remaining sides.

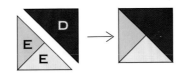

*Middle Border
Unit Diagram—Make 40.*

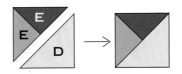

*Middle Border Corner
Unit Diagram—Make 4.*

6. Sew 1½"-wide red borders to quilt top.

ADDING OUTER BORDER

1. See General Instructions (page 169) for tips on mitered border corners. Join tan print borders to quilt top. Press seam allowances toward borders; then stitch corner seams.

2. See tip box (page 131) on Preparing Bias Strips for Appliqué. Following those instructions, prepare bias strips so they are ⅜" wide.

3. Fuse hearts to baskets. Center a basket over each mitered seam. Tuck ends of 2 bias strips under top edge of each basket. Fuse baskets in place.

4. Referring to photograph, baste vines in gentle curves along sides of quilt. Pin tulips and tulip tips at ends of vines at center of each quilt side, spacing tulips approximately 1" apart. (Trim ends of vines if necessary.) Fuse tulips and tulip tips in place.

5. Fuse 5 leaves, 4 cherries, 1 bird and wing, and 1 star flower and flower center along each vine as shown. Birds should face toward center of quilt sides.

6. See General Instructions (pages 166 and 167) for directions on buttonhole-stitch appliqué. Buttonhole-stitch around each appliqué piece by hand or by machine.

QUILTING AND FINISHING

1. Mark quilting designs on quilt top. On quilt shown, bird template was used to mark quilting design in C squares. For inner border, leaf template was used to mark leaves on either side of a ⅜"-wide vine.

2. Divide backing fabric into 2 (1⅝-yard) lengths. Cut 1 piece in half lengthwise. Discard 1 narrow panel. Sew remaining narrow panel to 1 side of wide panel.

3. Layer backing, batting, and quilt top; baste. Quilt as desired.

4. See General Instructions (page 174) for directions on making and applying binding. Make 220" of straight-grain binding.

5. See page 145 for directions on making a hanging sleeve.

Middle Border

Inner Border

Border Diagram

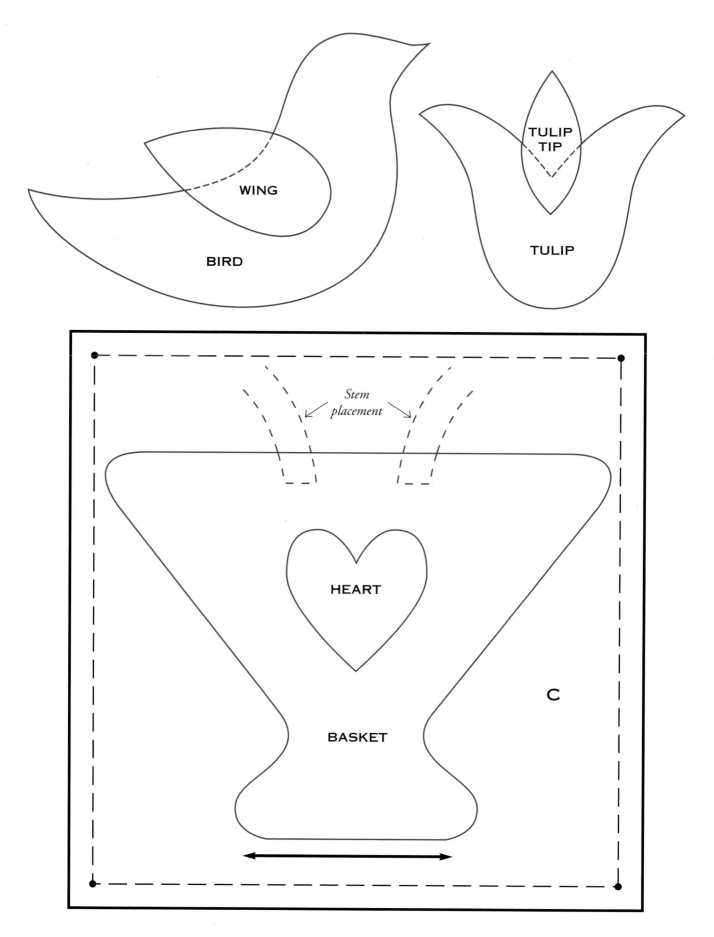

WING

BIRD

TULIP
TIP

TULIP

Stem placement

HEART

C

BASKET

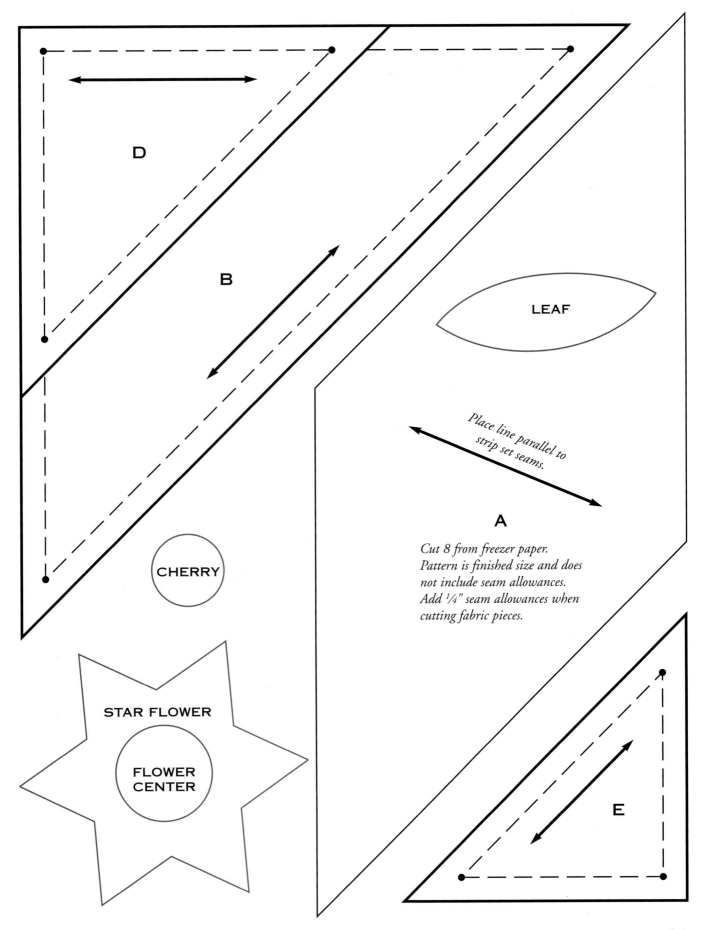

D

B

LEAF

Place line parallel to strip set seams.

A

*Cut 8 from freezer paper.
Pattern is finished size and does
not include seam allowances.
Add ¼" seam allowances when
cutting fabric pieces.*

CHERRY

STAR FLOWER

FLOWER
CENTER

E

GROWING UP WITH QUILTS

Quilts for children

hold a special place

in a quilter's heart.

We once met a

quilter who said,

"I was born into a quilt;

maybe that's why I

love them so much."

Four-in-Nine-Patch instructions begin on page 100.

WELCOME GIFTS FOR BABY

A little fabric goes a long way toward making a cozy crib quilt and handsome accessories for baby. The birth announcement and bear are created from scraps left over from the crib quilt, making a matching set that is fast and easy to sew.

A **FOUR-IN-NINE-PATCH** crib quilt combines homey plaids and friendly prints in simple patchwork that's ideal for a first-time quiltmaker. Fabrics are easy to coordinate in any color scheme to suit either baby girl or boy.

Paint, embroider, or cross-stitch a **BIRTH ANNOUNCEMENT** to set in a patchwork frame. Use leftover scraps to create an adorable **TEDDY BEAR** that's just right for little hands to hold and hearts to love.

Birth Announcement instructions begin on page 102.
Teddy Bear instructions begin on page 104.

95

ADORABLE APPLIQUÉ

Buttonhole-stitch embroidery highlights a crib quilt of **PAPER DOLLS**, dressed in scraps and surrounded by a field of pretty pastel hearts.

To make the appliqué easy, position the shapes with fusible webbing and stitch by machine. For handwork lovers, traditional appliqué methods will produce a lovely quilt to treasure forever.

This sweet quilt is perfect for a little girl, but boys are special too, and deserve quilts of their own. So we've included patterns for a boy doll and star, shown here in a pair of pillows, to inspire you to make a boy's version of the quilt.

Paper Doll Pillows instructions begin on page 110.

96

Paper Dolls instructions
begin on page 107.

QUILTS TO DREAM ON

When a baby is due, organize a shower that sends the mother-to-be home with a quilt full of good wishes. Quick-pieced and machine-quilted by friends, the cheerful **HOURGLASS** crib quilt is the perfect project for a joint effort among friends.

As children grow up, dreams turn to adventure. Michigan quilter Judy Walker Mead makes naptime at Grandma's a safari when her grandchildren go **SNOOZIN' WITH SNAKES**. Each of 15 whimsical snakes has an open-up mouth with a pocket inside to hold a love note or candy treat. The one snake headed in the "wrong" direction is a tribute to a red-headed grandchild who has a mind of her own!

Hourglass instructions begin on page 112.

Snoozin' with Snakes instructions begin on page 114.

FOUR-IN-NINE-PATCH

The Four-in-Nine-Patch block is a variation of the basic nine-patch.
The four-patch squares in these 12 blocks form chains that criss-cross the quilt.
Use strip piecing to assemble patches quickly and easily.

Finished size of quilt: 39" x 51"   **Finished size of block:** 9" square

MATERIALS

1⅛ yards of blue plaid fabric
1 yard of blue print fabric for sashing
⅝ yard of gold print fabric
⅝ yard of tan plaid fabric
1⅝ yards of backing fabric
45" x 60" (crib-size) precut batting
Rotary cutter, acrylic ruler, and
    cutting mat
Template plastic (optional)

CUTTING

For this crib quilt, strip-piecing makes fast work of the many four-patch units. If you prefer traditional cutting and piecing, make templates for patterns A and B on page 103. Refer to block diagrams to identify each piece by letter.

Save leftover fabrics to make the teddy bear shown on page 95. Instructions for the bear begin on page 104.

From blue plaid fabric, cut:

♥ 1 (21") square for bias binding.
♥ 8 (2"-wide) strips for four-patch
   units.

From blue print fabric, cut:

♥ 8 (3½"-wide) strips.
   From these, cut 31 (3½" x 9½")
   sashing strips.

From gold print fabric, cut:

♥ 8 (2"-wide) strips for four-patch
   units.

From tan plaid fabric, cut:

♥ 4 (3½"-wide) strips.
   From these, cut 48 (3½")
   B squares.

MAKING FOUR-PATCH UNITS

1. To strip-piece four-patch segments, join each blue plaid strip to a gold print strip as shown in *Strip Set Diagram*. Press seam allowances toward blue strip. Make 8 strip sets. From these, cut 160 (2"-wide) segments.

Strip Set Diagram

Four-Patch Diagram

2. To make four-patch segments traditionally, cut 160 A squares from blue plaid strips and 160 A squares from gold print strips. Join each gold A square to a blue A square. Press seam allowances toward blue squares.
3. Join 2 segments as shown in *Four-Patch Diagram*.
4. Make 80 four-patch units, 60 for blocks and 20 for sashing units.

MAKING FOUR-IN-NINE-PATCH BLOCKS

1. Referring to *Block Assembly Diagram*, arrange 5 four-patch units and 4 tan plaid B squares.
2. Join units in 3 vertical rows as shown. Press seam allowances toward B squares.
3. Join rows to complete block.
4. Repeat to make 12 blocks.

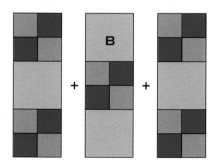

Block Assembly Diagram

Sashing Row Diagram

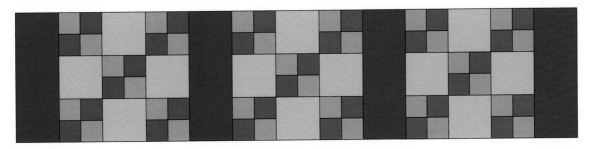

Block Row Diagram

QUILT ASSEMBLY

1. Join 3 sashing strips and 4 four-patch units in a horizontal row as shown in *Sashing Row Diagram.* Make 5 sashing rows. Press seam allowances toward sashing strips.

2. Join 3 blocks and 4 sashing strips in a row as shown in *Block Row Diagram.* Make 4 block rows. Press seam allowances toward sashing strips.

3. Alternating sashing rows and block rows, join rows as shown in photograph.

QUILTING AND FINISHING

1. Mark quilting designs on quilt top. The quilt shown has an X quilted through each four-patch unit and tan plaid square. Cookie-cutter stars are quilted in sashing strips.

2. Layer backing, batting, and quilt top; baste.

3. Quilt marked motifs and other quilting designs as desired.

4. Referring to tip box on page 18, make 190" of 2"-wide *continuous bias* binding from 21" square of plaid fabric. (If not using plaid fabric, you may prefer to make straight-grain binding.) See General Instructions (page 174) for directions on applying binding.

Designed and made by Liz Porter, 1991.

BIRTH ANNOUNCEMENT

Liz used fabrics left over from the crib quilt to frame a hand-painted birth announcement. Experiment with inexpensive water-based paints and permanent markers to create your own illustrated design. Or you might substitute tea-dyed cross-stitch for the painted muslin.

Finished size of patchwork: 10" x 10"

MATERIALS

¼ yard of muslin
⅛ yard of gold print fabric
⅛ yard of blue plaid fabric
Rotary cutter, acrylic ruler, and
    cutting mat
Permanent fabric marking pens
Acrylic paints and small paintbrushes
10" square of foam-core or artboard
    for mounting
Masking tape
Frame with 10"-square opening

CUTTING

For traditional cutting and piecing
methods, make a template for pattern
X below.

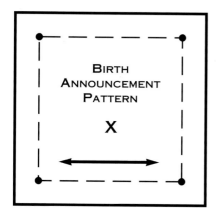

Designed and made by Liz Porter, 1994. Hand lettering by Jackie Leckband.

From muslin, cut:

❤ 1 (7") square for birth
    announcement.
❤ 2 (3" x 15½") mounting strips.
❤ 2 (3" x 10½") mounting strips.

From gold print and blue plaid fabrics, cut:

❤ 2 (1½"-wide) strips from *each*
    fabric.

PAINTING

Using permanent pens, acrylic paints, and small brushes, letter baby's name and birth information in center of muslin square as desired. Limit design area to 5½" square. Let dry.

To create the "antiqued" look of our announcement, make a thin paint wash by diluting brown paint with water; then brush paint over completed design. Blot with tissue to give mottled appearance. Let dry.

ASSEMBLY

1. Centering painted design, trim muslin to 6½" square.

2. To strip-piece borders, join each blue plaid strip to a gold print strip as shown in *Strip Set Diagram.* Press seam allowances toward blue strip. Make 2 strip sets. From these, cut 32 (1½"-wide) segments.

Strip Set Diagram

3. To make borders traditionally, cut 32 X squares from blue plaid strips and 32 X squares from gold print strips. Join each gold X square to a blue X square. Press seam allowances toward blue squares.

4. Referring to *Assembly Diagram,* join 6 segments to make top border. Repeat for bottom border. Join 10 segments to make each side border.

5. Sew shorter borders to top and bottom of muslin square. Press seam allowances toward center.

6. Sew 3" x 10½" muslin strips to side patchwork borders. Press seam allowances toward muslin. Referring to *Assembly Diagram,* sew side units to opposite sides of center unit. Press seam allowances toward center.

7. Sew 3" x 15½" muslin strips to top and bottom. Press seam allowances toward muslin.

MOUNTING

Center foam-core or artboard on back of birth announcement. Fold muslin strips over board and secure with masking tape. Insert mounted birth announcement in picture frame and secure with tape.

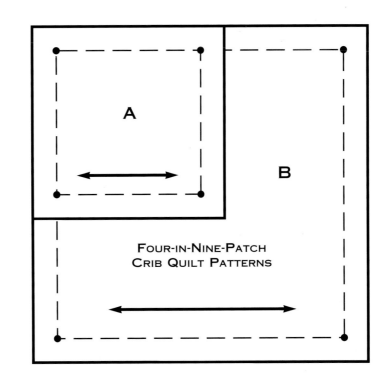

A

B

FOUR-IN-NINE-PATCH
CRIB QUILT PATTERNS

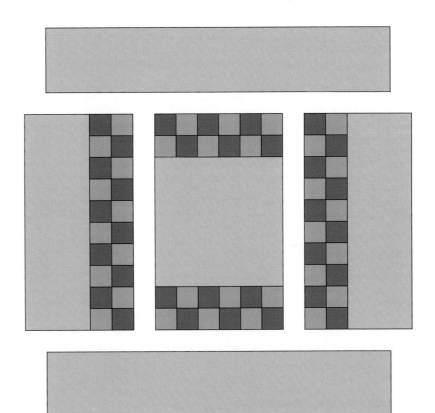

Assembly Diagram

TEDDY BEAR

This old-fashioned bear looks like it was made from pieces of an old quilt, but it is created from new fabrics. We joined two Nine-Patch blocks and 21 squares and machine-quilted them to make a "quilt." Then we washed it to make it look old before cutting the bear pieces.

Finished size of bear: Approximately 9" tall

From light-value scraps, cut:
❤ 8 (1¾") A squares for Nine-Patch blocks.

From assorted scraps, cut:
❤ 21 (4¼") B squares.

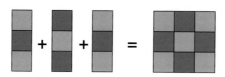

Nine-Patch Assembly Diagram

MAKING NINE-PATCH BLOCKS

1. Select 5 medium/dark A squares and 4 light A squares.

2. Referring to *Nine-Patch Assembly Diagram,* join squares in 3 rows, positioning light and dark values as shown. Press seam allowances toward darker fabrics.

3. Join rows to make 1 block.

4. Repeat to make 1 more Nine-Patch block.

MAKING PATCHWORK

1. Referring to *Patchwork Diagram,* join B squares and Nine-Patch blocks in diagonal rows. Press seam allowances in alternate directions from row to row.

2. Join rows.

3. Layer muslin, flannel, and patchwork; baste. Trim excess flannel and muslin, leaving at least 1" extra around patchwork.

4. Machine-quilt through each Nine-Patch and each B square as shown by dotted lines in *Patchwork Diagram.*

5. Machine-wash and dry quilted fabric 3 times if you want it to shrink and look old.

MATERIALS

Scraps of 12–15 fabrics of assorted light and dark values
½ yard of cotton flannel to layer between top and backing
½ yard of muslin for backing fabric
Polyester stuffing
Black pearl cotton and hand embroidery needle
¾ yard of ⅜"-wide ribbon
Rotary cutter, acrylic ruler, and cutting mat
Template plastic (optional)
Note: Do not prewash fabrics or flannel if you want your patchwork to shrink and look old after washing.

CUTTING

For traditional cutting, make templates for patterns A and B on page 106.

From medium/dark-value scraps, cut:
❤ 10 (1¾") A squares for Nine-Patch blocks.

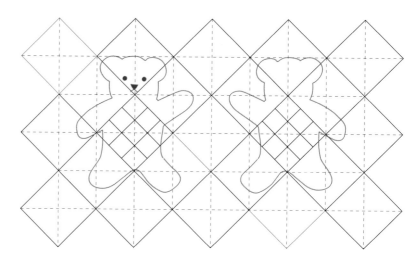

Patchwork Diagram

MAKING TEDDY BEAR

1. Make template of bear pattern.

2. Center template over 1 Nine-Patch and trace outline. Turn template over and center it on other Nine-Patch; trace. Cut out 2 bears.

3. Using pearl cotton, satin-stitch eyes and nose on 1 bear piece as shown on pattern. Add straight stitches for mouth.

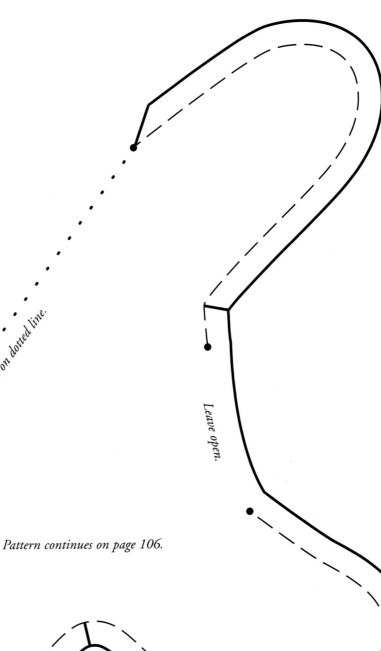

Satin Stitch

4. With right sides facing and raw edges aligned, pin bear pieces together. Stitch around bear, leaving a 2" opening as shown on pattern.

5. Clip seams and turn right side out. Stuff with polyester stuffing. Hand-stitch opening closed.

6. Tie ribbon around bear's neck.

Join pattern on dotted line.

Leave open.

Pattern continues on page 106.

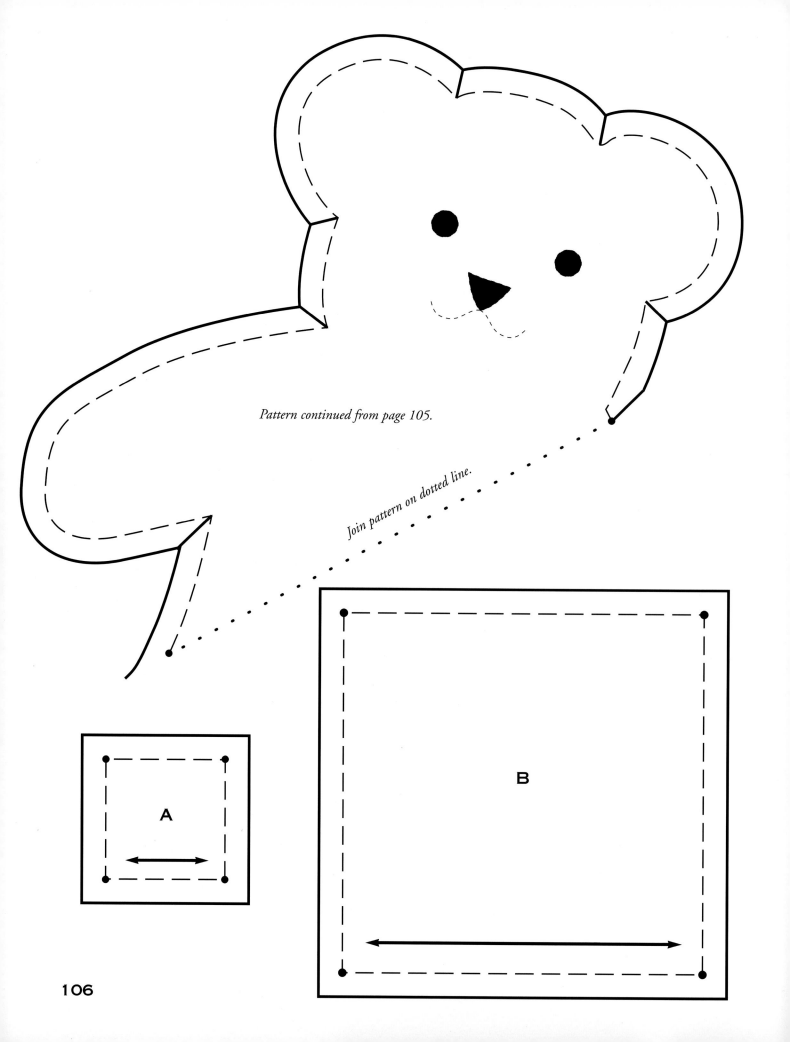

Pattern continued from page 105.

Join pattern on dotted line.

A

B

PAPER DOLLS

We fused appliqués and buttonhole-stitched each piece by machine to make 12 doll blocks and 12 candy-colored hearts. If you prefer, add decorative stitching by hand or use traditional hand appliqué techniques. For little boys, substitute patterns for boy doll and star on page 109.

Finished size of quilt: 34¾" x 51¼"   **Finished size of blocks:** 6½" square

MATERIALS

¾ yard *each* of 2 light print fabrics for background squares

¾ yard of pink checked fabric for sashing

½ yard of yellow fabric for sashing squares and binding

Assorted scraps for appliqués

1⅝ yards of backing fabric

45" x 60" (crib-size) precut batting

Rotary cutter, acrylic ruler, and cutting mat

1½ yards of paper-backed fusible webbing (optional)

Embroidery floss for hand embroidery (optional)

CUTTING

Before cutting, choose an appliqué technique for making this quilt. See General Instructions (pages 167 and 168) for tips on buttonhole-stitch appliqué and machine appliqué, noting information on preparing appliqués with fusible webbing.

(continued)

Designed and made by Marianne Fons and Liz Porter, 1994.

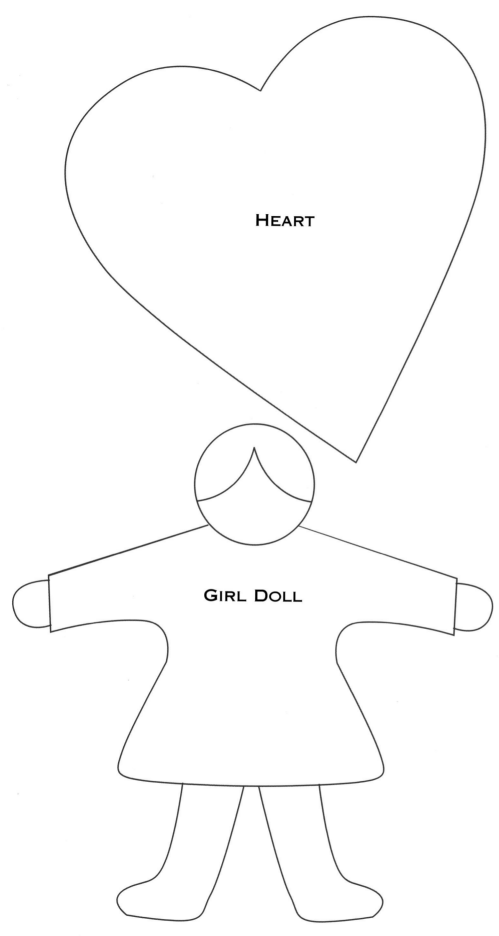

HEART

GIRL DOLL

Directions on preparing pieces for traditional hand appliqué are on page 166. For traditional appliqué, add seam allowances when cutting out pieces.

From *each* light print fabric, cut:
❤ 2 (7"-wide) strips.
From these, cut 24 (7") background squares.

From pink checked fabric, cut:
❤ 10 (2¼"-wide) strips.
From these, cut 58 (2¼" x 7") sashing strips.

From yellow fabric, cut:
❤ 2 (2¼"-wide) strips.
From these, cut 35 (2¼") sashing squares.
❤ 5 (2"-wide) binding strips.

From assorted scraps, cut:
❤ 12 *each* of heart, dress, hair, face, right hand, left hand, right leg, and left leg.

APPLIQUÉING BLOCKS
1. Fold each background square in half vertically and lightly crease to make a center guideline.

2. For each heart block, center a heart on guideline. Position top cleft 1½" below top edge of square. Fuse or pin heart in place. Prepare 12 heart blocks.

3. For each doll block, center doll pieces on guideline. Position top of doll's hair ⅞" from top edge of square. Fuse or pin pieces in place. Prepare 12 doll blocks.

4. Machine- or hand-stitch edges of appliqué pieces to make 24 blocks. For hand buttonhole-stitch, use 2 strands of floss. (See page 167 for stitch diagram.) For machine button-hole-stitch, refer to machine manual for settings. *Machine Stitching Diagram* shows sequence and direction for stitching doll appliqués—for each piece, begin stitching at number and work around as indicated by arrows.

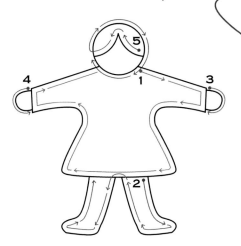

Machine Stitching Diagram

QUILT ASSEMBLY

Referring to photograph, arrange 6 horizontal rows of blocks and sashing strips, positioning doll and heart blocks as shown. Between block rows, lay out 7 rows of alternating sashing strips and squares.

Join pieces in each row. Press all seam allowances toward sashing strips. Join rows.

QUILTING AND FINISHING

1. Layer backing, batting, and quilt top; baste.

2. The quilt shown was outline-quilted by machine. An X is quilted through each sashing square. Quilt as desired.

3. See General Instructions (page 174) for directions on making and applying binding. Make 175" of straight-grain binding.

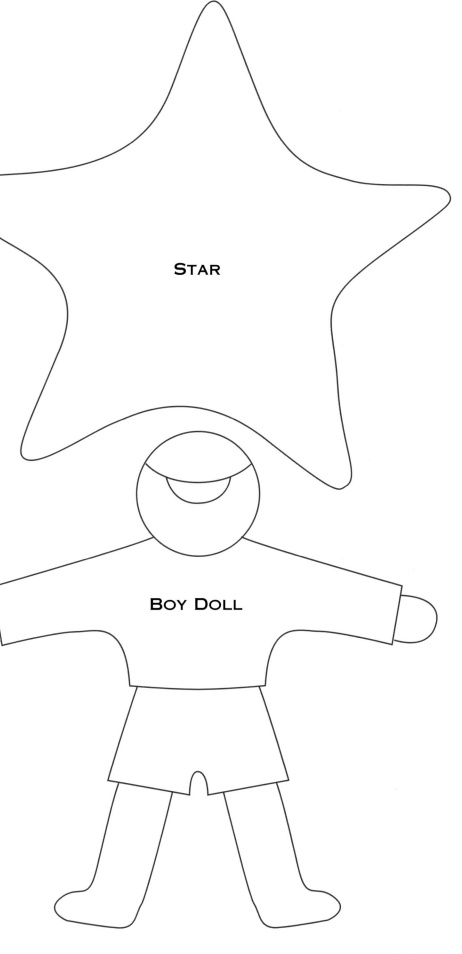

STAR

BOY DOLL

PAPER DOLL PILLOWS

Little boys need quilts, too, so the boy doll and star patterns can stand in for the girl and heart in the crib quilt. For this pair of pillows, fusible webbing and machine buttonhole-stitching make the job fast and easy. If you prefer, add buttonhole-stitch by hand or use traditional hand-appliqué methods.

Finished size of pillows: 9½" square   **Finished size of blocks:** 6½"

MATERIALS

⅓ yard of cream fabric for pillow
  fronts and backs
1 (2"-wide) strip *each* of 2 blue
  fabrics for borders
1 (10") square of fabric for bias
  cording
Assorted scraps for appliqué
2½ yards of ¼"-diameter cording
Polyester stuffing
Rotary cutter, acrylic ruler, and
  cutting mat
¼ yard of paper-backed fusible
  webbing (optional)
Embroidery floss and hand
  sewing needle (optional)
Template plastic (optional)

CUTTING

Before cutting, choose an appliqué technique for this project. See General Instructions (pages 167 and 168) for tips on buttonhole-stitch appliqué and machine appliqué, noting information on preparing appliqués with fusible webbing. Directions on preparing pieces for traditional hand appliqué are on page 166. For traditional appliqué, add seam allowances when cutting pieces. Appliqué patterns are on pages 108 and 109.

Pillows made by Mabeth Oxenreider of Carlisle, Iowa, 1994.

From cream fabric, cut:
❤ 2 (11") squares for pillow backs.
❤ 2 (7") squares for pillow fronts.

From *each* border fabric, cut:
❤ 2 (2" x 7") strips.
❤ 2 (2" x 10") strips.

From assorted scraps, cut:
❤ 1 *each* of star, shirt, shorts, cap,
  hair, face, right hand, left hand,
  right leg, and left leg.

MAKING BLOCKS

To prepare and stitch appliqué blocks, follow instructions given for Making Blocks for *Paper Dolls.* Make 1 boy block and 1 star block.

PILLOW ASSEMBLY

1. Sew a 7"-long border strip to 2 opposite sides of each block. Press seam allowances toward borders. Sew 10"-long strips to remaining edges.

2. See page 18 for tips on making continuous bias. From 10" square, make 90" of 1"-wide bias.

3. With wrong sides facing, fold bias in half lengthwise. Using a zipper foot, machine-baste bias around cording.

4. With raw edges aligned, baste cording to right side of each pillow front. Where ends overlap, let them extend over raw edge of pillow front.

5. With right sides facing and cording sandwiched between, pin pillow front to back. Stitch front to back, leaving a 2"-wide opening in 1 side for turning.

6. Trim seam allowances and clip corners as necessary. Turn pillow right side out and stuff firmly. Hand-sew opening closed.

MAKING QUICK-PIECED HOURGLASS BLOCKS

When making several Hourglass blocks from the same two-fabric combination, it's much faster and more accurate to quick-piece the blocks than to cut and sew individual triangles. Here's an easy method for making Hourglass blocks in minutes!

1. Cut a square of each fabric that is 1¼" larger than the desired *finished* size of the block. For our Hourglass crib quilt, cut 7¼" squares. You will get 2 Hourglass blocks from each set of matching squares.

2. On wrong side of lighter-colored square, draw diagonal lines from corner to corner in *both* directions. With right sides facing, match marked square with square of second fabric.

3. Referring to *Diagram 1*, stitch ¼" seam on *both* sides of 1 diagonal line. Press stitching.

4. Referring to *Diagram 2*, cut units apart on line between stitching. Press units open, pressing seam allowance toward darker fabric. You will have 2 triangle-squares as shown in *Diagram 3*.

5. On wrong side of 1 triangle-square, extend drawn line from corner of light triangle to corner of dark triangle. Then match both triangle-squares with contrasting fabrics facing and marked unit on top.

6. Referring to *Diagram 4*, stitch ¼" seam on *both* sides of marked line.

7. Referring to *Diagram 5*, cut units apart between stitching lines as before. Press both units open to get 2 Hourglass blocks as shown in *Diagram 6*. In our example, blocks will measure 6½" square (including seam allowances). When joined, finished size of blocks will be 6" square.

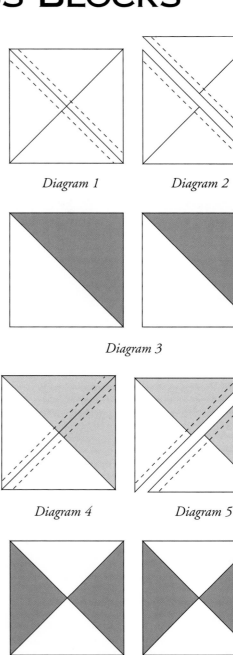

Diagram 1   *Diagram 2*

Diagram 3

Diagram 4   *Diagram 5*

Diagram 6

HOURGLASS

Quick-piece this merry pattern for a colorful gift. (See the tip box on page 113 on how to use this crib quilt as the focal point for a quilter's baby shower.) We used the method for Hourglass blocks explained on page 111, mixing bright solids with a confetti print to make 35 blocks.

Finished size of quilt: 37½" x 49½"   **Finished size of block:** 6" square

MATERIALS

1¼ yards of white print fabric
¾ yard of teal fabric for patchwork
    and outer border
¾ yard of gold fabric for patchwork
    and binding
¼ yard *each* of fuchsia, green, and
    purple fabrics
1½ yards of backing fabric
45" x 60" (crib-size) precut batting
Rotary cutter, acrylic ruler, and
    cutting mat

CUTTING

The following instructions are for quick-piecing technique explained on page 111. If you prefer traditional cutting and piecing, make a template of A triangle on page 117.

From white print fabric, cut:

❤ 4 (1½"-wide) strips for inner
    border.

❤ 4 (7¼"-wide) strips.
    From these, cut 20 (7¼") squares.

From teal fabric, cut:
- 4 (3¼"-wide) strips for outer border.

From gold fabric, cut:
- 5 (2"-wide) strips for binding.

From teal, gold, fuchsia, green, and purple fabrics, cut:
- 1 (7¼"-wide) strip of *each* fabric. From each strip, cut 4 (7¼") squares.

From fuchsia fabric, cut:
- 4 (3¼") squares for border corners.

MAKING BLOCKS

Follow instructions for Hourglass blocks on page 111, combining a print square with each solid square. You will make 8 blocks of each color combination. For a quilt like ours, set aside 1 block of each color. Use the extra blocks to make matching pillows or other crib accessories.

QUILT ASSEMBLY

1. Referring to photograph, arrange 35 Hourglass blocks in 7 horizontal rows, placing 1 block of each color in each row and turning them as shown. Join blocks into rows. Join rows.
2. Measure length through middle of quilt. Trim 2 print border strips to this length (approximately 42½"). Sew borders to quilt sides.
3. Measure width of quilt in same manner, including side borders. Trim remaining print borders to this length (approximately 32½"). Sew these borders to top and bottom edges of quilt.
4. Measure length of quilt top again, including seam allowances. Trim 2 teal borders to this length (approximately 44½"). (If yardage is narrow, you may have to cut another strip and piece borders to achieve needed length.) Measure width of quilt top, including seam allowances. Trim remaining teal borders to this length (approximately 32½").
5. Sew longer borders to quilt sides. Press seam allowances toward borders.
6. Sew a corner square to each end of remaining borders. Press seam allowances toward borders. Sew borders to top and bottom edges of quilt.

QUILTING AND FINISHING

1. Layer backing, batting, and quilt top; baste.
2. Quilt as desired. The quilt shown was machine-quilted in-the-ditch with mock-Hourglass blocks quilted in outer border.
3. See General Instructions (page 174) for directions on making and applying binding. Make 185" of straight-grain binding.

HOST A MAKE-A-QUILT BABY SHOWER

Quilting friends can't find enough ways to quilt together, so here's another fun suggestion. Get your group involved in making a crib quilt *during* the baby shower. With a little planning, you can give the new baby a wonderful memento of mom's quiltmaking friends.

Along with the invitations, mail two fabric squares and the simple instructions on page 111 for making Hourglass blocks. Each guest follows these steps to

make two blocks to bring to the party.

Set up a sewing machine in a corner of the party room. While the guest-of-honor is opening gifts, you and your guests can take turns sewing blocks together. At the party's end, you'll have a completed quilt top, ready to tie or machine-quilt. Present the finished quilt to the mother-to-be before the baby is born or deliver it to the hospital in time for the baby's trip home.

SNOOZIN' WITH SNAKES

Quick cutting is ideal for the many triangles in this quilt. The heads are made separately and hand-sewn to the quilt after quilting and binding are complete. Judy used dotted fabric for the snakes' eyes, but you can use a permanent marker to draw eyes on solid fabric.

Finished size of quilt: 67" x 97"

MATERIALS

3⅝ yards of black dotted fabric for background

½ yard *each* of 2 coordinating striped fabrics for border

½ yard *each* of 15 print fabrics for snakes

Scraps of solid fabrics for eyes

6 yards of coordinating fabric for backing and mock binding

⅜ yard of fleece for heads

90" x 108" (queen-size) precut batting

Rotary cutter, acrylic ruler, and cutting mat

Plastic-coated freezer paper

Template plastic

Black permanent marking pen for eyes

15 (⅝"-diameter) Velcro dots (optional)

CUTTING

For traditional cutting and piecing methods, make templates for patterns A and B on page 117. Refer to diagrams to identify each piece by letter.

Even if you are using a rotary cutter, you will need a template for pattern A if you use any striped fabrics (Judy's quilt has two). Mark and cut those fabrics with a template so the stripes run in the right direction.

From *each* of 15 prints, cut:

❤ 1 (7¼"-wide) strip.
From this, cut 5 (7¼") squares. Cut each square diagonally in *both* directions to get 19 A triangles and 1 extra of each fabric. (For striped fabrics, cut 2 strips and cut traditionally with long side of triangle template parallel to stripe.)

❤ 2 (6½") squares for head.

❤ 1 (3" x 6") piece for head pocket.

❤ 1 (3⅞") square from 8 fabrics only. Cut square in half diagonally to get 1 B triangle and 1 extra.

From striped border fabrics, cut:

❤ 9 (2½"-wide) strips, cutting 6 strips from first fabric and 3 strips from second fabric.

From background fabric, cut:

❤ 15 (7¼"-wide) strips.
From these, cut 72 (7¼") squares. Cut each square diagonally in *both* directions to get 285 A triangles and 3 extra.

❤ 3 (3⅞"-wide) strips.
From these, cut 26 (3⅞") squares. Cut each square in half diagonally to get 52 B triangles.

From fleece, cut:

❤ 15 (6½") squares for heads.

PIECING SNAKES

This quilt has 2 types of snakes, each consisting of 2 rows of patchwork.

1. For each Snake X, select 19 background A triangles, 3 background B triangles, and 19 A triangles and 1 B triangle from the same print fabric.

2. Referring to *Snake X Diagram*, arrange pieces for Row 1 and Row 2. Join triangles to make each row.

(continued)

Row 1
Row 2

Snake X Diagram—Make 8.

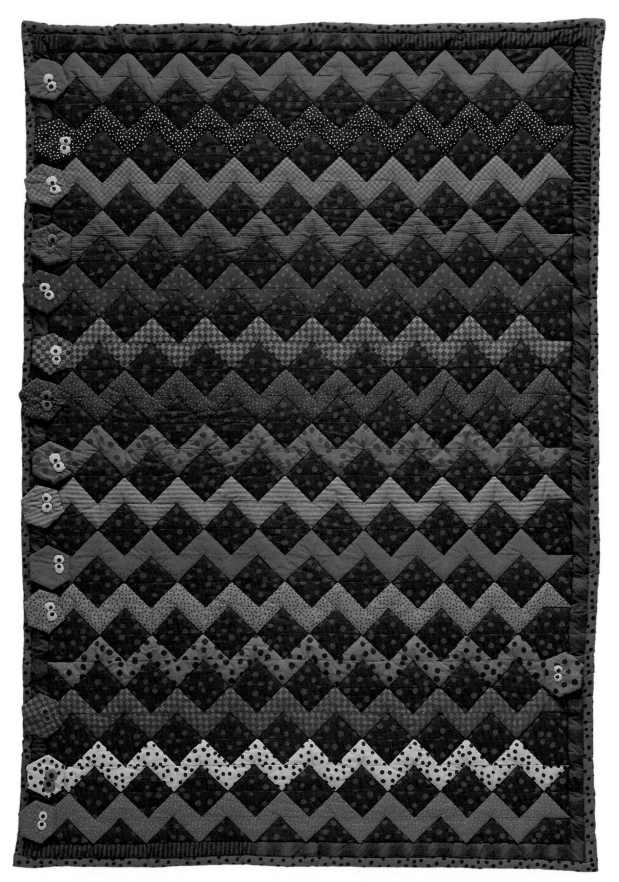

Designed and made by Judy Walker Mead of Lansing, Michigan, for her grandchildren, 1992.

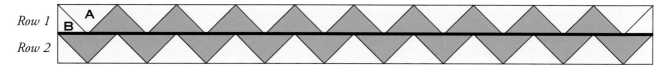

Row 1
Row 2

Snake Y Diagram—Make 7.

3. Before joining rows, mark center on long edge of each print A triangle. Join rows, matching center marks with points of background triangles in opposite row. Make 8 of Snake X.

4. For each Snake Y, select 19 background A triangles, 4 background B triangles, and 19 A triangles from 1 print fabric.

5. Referring to *Snake Y Diagram,* arrange pieces for Row 1 and Row 2. Join triangles to make each row.

6. Mark print triangles as before. Join rows. Make 7 of Snake Y.

Quilt Assembly

1. Referring to quilt photograph, arrange 15 snakes in horizontal rows, alternating X and Y types. Join rows.

2. Measure length of quilt, measuring through middle rather than along sides. Combining different lengths of 2 fabrics as desired, join border strips end-to-end to make 2 borders to match measured length (approximately 90½"). Sew borders to quilt sides, easing as necessary.

3. Measure width through middle of quilt top. Assemble 2 borders to match this measurement (approximately 64½"). Join these borders to top and bottom edges of quilt.

Quilting and Binding

1. Divide backing fabric into 2 (3-yard) lengths. Cut 1 piece in half lengthwise. Sew a narrow panel to each side of wide panel.

2. Layer backing, batting, and quilt top; baste.

3. Quilt as desired. The quilt shown is outline-quilted.

4. Using rotary cutter and ruler, trim backing and batting so they are 3½" larger than quilt top. Using scissors, trim batting again so it is 1½" larger than quilt top. Save excess batting for stuffing snake eyes.

5. On all sides, turn in ½" on raw edge of backing. Fold backing over edge to front of quilt, enclosing raw edges of batting, quilt top, and backing. Topstitch through all layers.

Making Snake Heads

1. Trace head pattern on page 117 onto non-waxed side of freezer paper. Cut out *finished-size* template. Be sure to transfer Xs to paper template.

2. For head, select 2 matching squares of fabric and 1 fleece square. Using a dry iron, center and press paper template, shiny side down, on *wrong* side of 1 fabric square.

3. With right sides facing and paper template facing you, layer 2 matching squares. Place fleece underneath, against fabric square without pattern. Pin layers together, pinning through paper pattern.

4. Starting with a backstitch at first X, machine-stitch through all layers along edge of paper pattern. (Do not stitch through paper, but use edge of pattern as a sewing guide.) Backstitch where seam ends at second X.

5. Leaving ¼" for seam allowances, trim excess fabric and fleece. Remove paper pattern. Turn head right side out and hand-sew opening closed.

6. Repeat steps 1–5 to make 15 snake heads. You should be able to reuse paper templates for 2 or 3 heads.

7. Finished eyes are 1"–1½" in diameter. Cut 30 assorted circles for eyes twice desired finished size, or 2"–3" in diameter. Mark pupils on fabric with a permanent pen.

8. Run a basting thread around each circle, ¼" from edge. Pull basting thread to gather, inserting wisps of batting for filler. Hand-appliqué eyes to heads, placing eyes as desired.

9. Hand-stitch back edge of each head to end of matching snake row on quilt. Position heads at alternating ends of snakes or all on same side of quilt, as desired. Judy's quilt has just 1 snake swimming against the tide.

Finishing

With right sides facing, fold each 3" x 6" pocket rectangle in half to make a 3" square. Sew a ¼" seam around edge, leaving a 1" opening for turning. Turn right side out and press. Hand-stitch opening closed.

Hand-sew 3 sides of matching pocket to underside of each head. If desired, sew Velcro dots to bottom of heads and to quilt border.

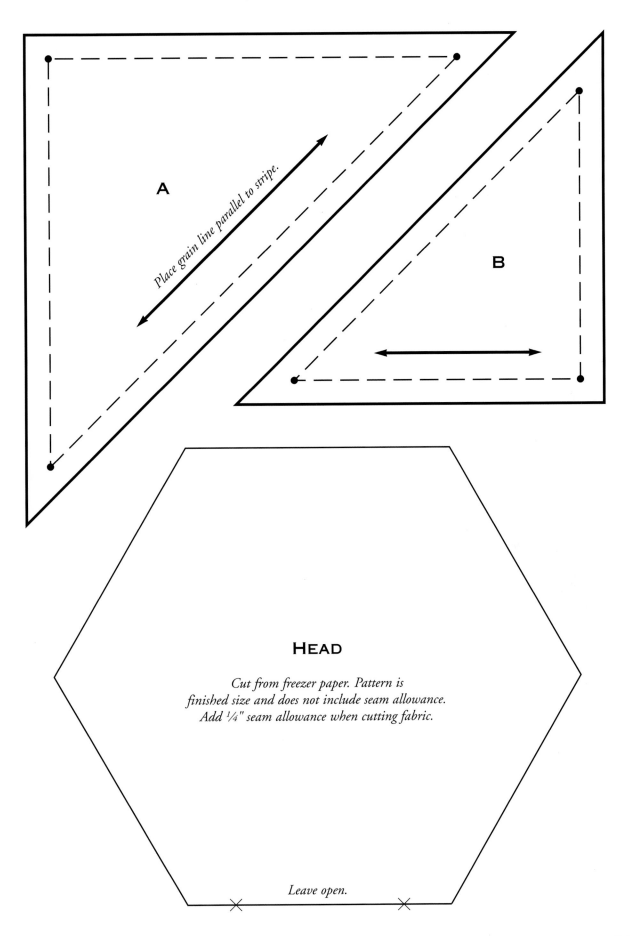

A

Place grain line parallel to stripe.

B

HEAD

*Cut from freezer paper. Pattern is
finished size and does not include seam allowance.
Add ¼" seam allowance when cutting fabric.*

Leave open.

Ann Poindexter   Nancy John   Mary Alice Stack

CELEBRATE THE SEASONS WITH QUILTS

To everything there

is a season,

and for every season

there is a quilt

that celebrates

your favorite time

of the year.

SEASONS' GREETINGS

Celebrate spring's arrival with a quilt of abundant appliquéd flowers in your favorite colors. Marianne chose a variety of blues and purples for her **SPRING BLOSSOMS**. Its bright colors and energetic curves embody the joy of spring after a cold Iowa winter.

Old Glory and a Sousa march inspired Liz to make **STARS AND STRIPES FOREVER!** To honor Independence Day, she chose two easy-to-piece blocks that alternate to form an interweaving geometric pattern in patriotic red, white, and blue.

Spring Blossoms **instructions begin on page 128.**

Stars and Stripes Forever! instructions
begin on page 134.

School Days instructions begin
on page 138.

HALCYON DAYS

As symbolic of autumn as falling leaves, caravans of yellow school buses herald the change of season. Children sharpen pencils, pack book bags, and go off to school. **SCHOOL DAYS** is a heart-warming quilt that was a retirement gift for Caroline Overton, a veteran of 31 years as a first-grade teacher. Caroline's colleagues helped make the quilt, adding appliquéd and embroidered details to personalize the blocks.

Fall is also harvest time, when crisp, shiny apples fill bushel baskets everywhere. Iowa quilter Cheryl Mathre pays tribute to her favorite fruit in **AUTUMN APPLES**, a cheerful wall hanging that can be made traditionally or with quick piecing techniques.

Autumn Apples **instructions begin on page 144.**

VISIONS OF

Hung by the chimney with care, **FOLK ART STOCKINGS** bring a primitive-style country air to Christmas festivities. Iowa folk artist Jackie Leckband used buttonhole stitches to appliqué selected motifs to these charming stockings. Working with wool eliminates

CHRISTMAS

the tedium of turning edges, and the decorative stitching is a perfect complement to the rich solid colors of the wool. Choose from our full-size patterns for appliqué motifs or create your own to arrange on the stocking background as desired.

Folk Art Stockings instructions begin on page 148.

FROST AND FESTIVITIES

When Jack Frost nips at your nose, our little **SNOWMAN** makes a cute tabletop decoration. He fits in with Christmas displays, but he'll also add to the coziness of home through all the winter months.

Count the days of December with a miniature quilt block for every day until Christmas. On Christmas Eve, your **ADVENT CALENDAR** will be completely filled in to cheer you through the

new year. Fabric corners, like paper ones used to mount photos in an album, hold each block in place.

To make the miniature blocks, choose from the patterns in our Bonus 3" Blocks section (page 78).

Snowman **instructions begin on page 153.**

Advent Calendar instructions begin on page 154.

SPRING BLOSSOMS

Marianne used purple and blue fabrics to machine-appliqué 12 floral blocks and the graceful swag borders that make this a challenging appliqué project. (You can stitch by hand if you prefer.) You'll find full-size patterns for the elegant feather quilting motifs on page 176.

Finished size of quilt: 81" x 100½"   **Finished size of block:** 18" square

MATERIALS

7½ yards of ivory solid fabric for
  background and binding

2 yards *each* of 3 print fabrics (purple,
  medium blue, and dark blue) for
  border swags

1⅛ yards of green fabric for stems
  and leaves

⅓ yard *each* of 15 purple and blue
  print fabrics for flowers and sawtooth sashing

Scraps of assorted yellow fabrics for
  flower stamens

6 yards of backing fabric or 3 yards of
  90"-wide muslin

90" x 108" (queen-size) precut batting

Rotary cutter, acrylic ruler, and
  cutting mat

Template plastic

Plastic-coated freezer paper

⅜"-wide bias bar for stems

Nonpermanent chalk or fabric pencil

Black permanent marker

CUTTING

Refer to General Instructions (pages 166 and 168) for tips on making templates and cutting pieces for hand or machine appliqué. Make plastic or freezer-paper templates for appliqué patterns on pages 132 and 133. For flowers, make separate templates for each flower part (A–D). For swags, make separate templates for top, middle, and bottom sections.

From ivory fabric, cut:

❤ 1 (2½-yard) piece.
  From this, cut 4 (11" x 83") *lengthwise* strips for borders. If fabric is not a full 44" wide, cut 8 crossgrain strips instead and join 2 strips end-to-end to get 4 strips of needed length.

❤ 1 (30") square for bias binding.

❤ 12 (19") squares for blocks. (Squares will be trimmed after appliqué is completed.)

❤ 12 (2⅜"-wide) strips.
  From these, cut 196 (2⅜") squares. Cut each square in half diagonally to get 392 triangles for sawtooth sashing.

From green print fabric, cut:

❤ 1 (24") square.
  From this, cut 24 (1⅛" x 13") bias strips for stems.

❤ 132 leaves.

From swag fabrics, cut:

❤ 14 *each* of top, middle, and bottom border swags. Marianne used purple fabric for top, medium blue fabric for middle, and dark blue fabric for bottom swag.

❤ 4 *each* of top, middle, and bottom corner swags. Add leftover swag fabrics to purple and blue fabrics for flowers and sawtooth sashing.

From assorted purple and blue fabrics, cut:

❤ 12 (2⅜"-wide) strips.
  From these, cut 196 (2⅜") squares. Cut each square in half diagonally to get 392 triangles for sawtooth sashing.

❤ 66 blue or purple A flower pieces.

❤ 66 purple C flower pieces.

❤ 66 blue or purple D flower pieces.

From assorted yellow fabrics, cut:

❤ 66 B flower pieces.

(continued)

Designed and made by Marianne Fons, 1994.
Machine-quilted by Fern Stewart.

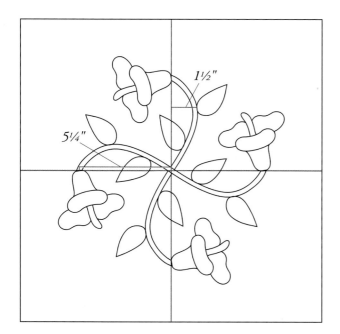

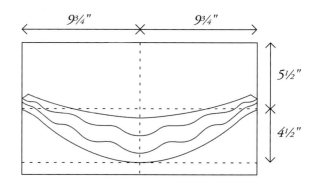

Swag Master Pattern Diagram

Block Diagram

APPLIQUÉING BLOCKS

1. Using plastic templates for flower pieces and referring to dimensions shown on *Block Diagram,* trace a master pattern on paper side of a 19" square of freezer paper. Darken placement lines with black marker.

2. Fold a 19" ivory square in half vertically and horizontally. Finger-press folds to make center guidelines. Aligning edges and centers, position square over master pattern. With chalk or pencil, *lightly* trace design onto fabric. Mark 12 blocks.

3. Using appliqué method of your choice, prepare pieces for 48 flowers and 96 leaves.

4. Referring to tip box on page 131, prepare 24 (13"-long) stems.

5. Starting with stems, pin or baste appliqué pieces in place on each block. Flower pieces are positioned in alphabetical order.

6. Stitch appliqué pieces in place on 12 blocks. Remove pins and basting as you work.

7. Measuring 9¼" from center on all sides, trim blocks to 18½" square.

QUILT ASSEMBLY WITH SAWTOOTH SASHING

1. Join each colored triangle to an ivory triangle to make 392 triangle-squares. Press seam allowances toward colored fabrics.

2. Positioning colored triangles at bottom right of each triangle-square, join 40 squares end-to-end to make a horizontal sashing strip. Make 5 horizontal sashing strips.

3. Positioning colored triangles at bottom left of each triangle-square, join 12 squares in same manner to make a vertical sashing strip. Make 16 vertical sashing strips.

4. Referring to photograph for positioning of sashing, join 4 vertical sashing strips and 3 blocks to make a horizontal row. Make 4 horizontal rows. Press seam allowances toward blocks.

5. Referring to photograph, join horizontal rows, alternating sashing strips with block rows. Press seam allowances toward blocks.

MAKING SIDE SWAG BORDERS

1. To make a master pattern, cut an 11" x 19½" piece of freezer paper. On paper side, draw a vertical and a horizontal line for center guidelines. Draw another placement line parallel to long edge, 1" from bottom. Referring to *Swag Master Pattern Diagram,* align bottom of swag pattern on page 133 with bottom placement line on paper and match pattern fold line with vertical center. Trace half-swag onto paper. Fold paper in half vertically to trace second half of swag. Darken lines of completed master pattern with black marker.

2. Measure length of quilt top, measuring through middle rather than at edges. Trim 1 ivory border strip to this length (approximately 80"). Fold border strip in half horizontally and vertically, finger-pressing folds to make guidelines. Starting from center of strip, measure 19½"-wide segments along length of border, marking each segment with a pin at bottom edge.

3. Aligning edges and horizontal center lines, position first border segment over master pattern. Pattern should fit precisely within pinned guidelines. With chalk or pencil, *lightly* trace swag onto fabric. Move

PREPARING BIAS STRIPS FOR APPLIQUÉ

The flower stems in *Spring Blossoms* are made with bias strips. We also used bias pieces—joined into a long strip—to make the vine in the *String Star* border. Bias pressing bars, made of metal or heat-resistant plastic, are convenient for preparing bias for appliqué. Sold in sets of three widths, pressing bars are available at quilt shops and from mail-order sources.

We usually rotary-cut bias strips from a fabric square. Instructions for projects tell you what size fabric square is required for stems or vines.

1. Fold in a corner of fabric square at a 45° angle and press lightly to crease.

2. Use ruler and rotary cutter to cut bias strips parallel to creased line *(Photo A)*. We cut strips 1⅛" wide for both *Spring Blossoms* and *String Star* for ⅜"-wide finished stems and vines.

3. To make a bias strip long enough for a continuous vine, join strips with diagonal seams as shown in General Instructions (page 174).

4. With wrong sides facing and raw edges aligned, fold strips in half lengthwise. Machine-stitch ⅛" from raw edges, making a narrow tube.

5. Slide a ⅜"-wide pressing bar into tube. Adjust strip to center seam on flat side of bar and press *(Photo B)*. Turn bar over and press other side. Slide bar through until entire strip is pressed. (Use caution when handling metal bars—they get hot!) Remove pressing bar.

6. With seam side against background fabric, baste or pin bias strips in place *(Photo C)*, using either placement lines marked on background fabric or a master pattern placed under block or border strip. Start each bias strip in a position where another piece will cover raw end.

7. Appliqué both sides of strips. Stitch inner curves first and then outer curves so that bias will lie flat.

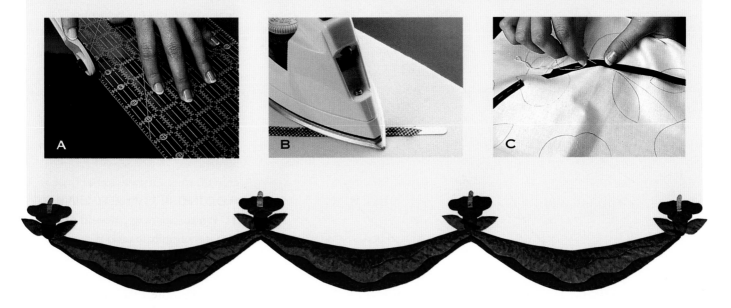

fabric to align next border segment with master pattern. In this manner, mark 4 swags on side border.

4. Pin bottom swags in place on border segments. Overlap swag ends where they meet. Pin middle and top swags in place in same manner. When satisfied with placement, appliqué swags in place.

5. Prepare appliqués for 3 flowers and 6 leaves. Pin a flower in place at intersections of top swags, placing leaves at each side of flower. Appliqué flowers and leaves on border.

6. Repeat steps 2–5 to make second side border.

7. Sew completed borders to quilt sides. Appliquéd flowers should align with horizontal sashing. Press seam allowances toward borders.

(continued)

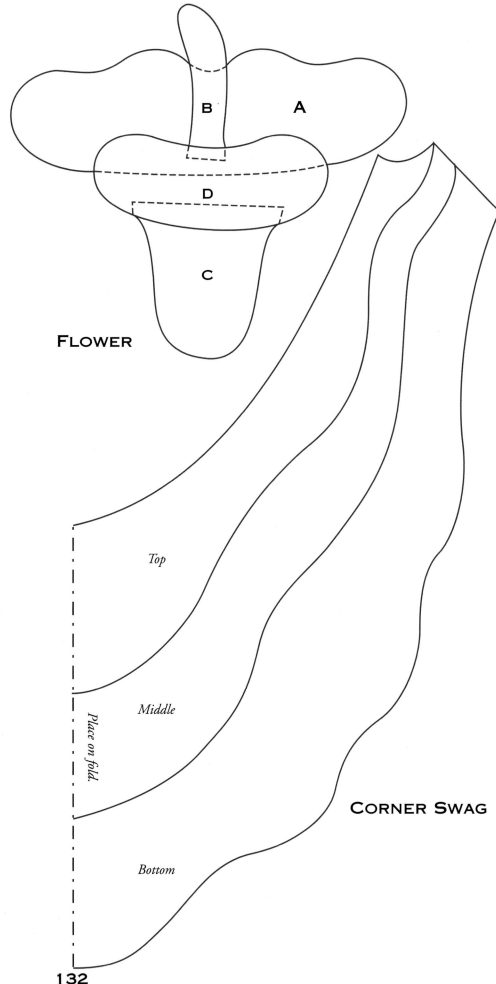

FLOWER

A
B
C
D

Top

Middle

Bottom

Place on fold.

CORNER SWAG

MAKING TOP AND BOTTOM SWAG BORDERS

1. Measure width of quilt top through middle rather than at edges. Trim 1 remaining border strip to this length (approximately 81½"). Fold border strip in half horizontally and vertically, finger-pressing folds to make guidelines.

2. Measure 9¾" to each side of center to mark first border segment. Mark 1 more 19½"-wide segment on each side of center segment.

3. Aligning edges and horizontal center lines, position border over master pattern and trace 3 swags onto fabric.

4. Pin swags in place on border as before. When satisfied with placement, appliqué swags in place.

5. Prepare appliqués for 2 flowers and 4 leaves. Pin a flower at intersections of top swags as before and appliqué in place.

6. Repeat steps 1–5 to make bottom border.

7. Sew completed borders to top and bottom edges of quilt. Appliquéd flowers should align with vertical sashing. Press seam allowances toward borders.

ADDING CORNER SWAGS

1. Pin corner swag pieces in place at 1 corner of quilt so ends slightly overlap swags on both sides. Due to variances of individual sewing, swags may not align precisely. Adjust corner swag as necessary and appliqué in place. Repeat for remaining corners.

2. Referring to photograph, appliqué flowers and leaves at ends of corner swags. Do not cut border curves until after binding is applied.

QUILTING AND FINISHING

1. Divide backing fabric into 2 (3-yard) lengths. Cut 1 piece in half lengthwise. Sew a narrow panel to each side of wide panel. Press seam allowances toward narrow panels.

2. Mark quilting designs on quilt top. Patterns for feathered quilting motifs used in block corners and borders are on page 176. The quilt shown also has outline quilting around appliqué pieces.

3. Layer backing, batting, and quilt top; baste. Quilt as desired.

4. Measure ½" from bottom of swags around quilt, making pencil marks for binding placement. Connect marks lightly with pencil to form sewing guideline.

5. Referring to tip box on page 18, make 450" of 2"-wide *continuous bias* binding from 30" square of ivory fabric.

6. See General Instructions (page 174) for directions on applying binding. Aligning raw edge of binding with marked line, sew binding to quilt.

7. Trim border fabric to binding seam allowance. Turn binding to quilt back and hand-finish.

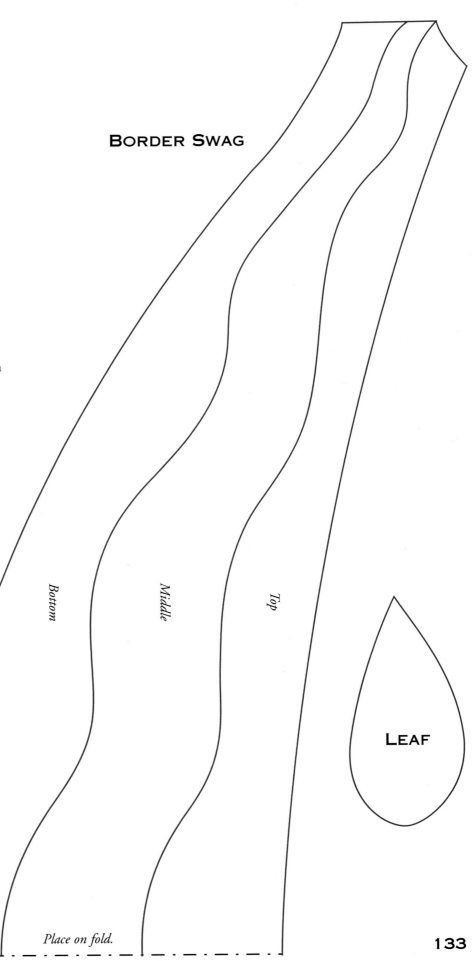

BORDER SWAG

Bottom

Middle

Top

LEAF

Place on fold.

STARS AND STRIPES FOREVER!

Old Glory was the inspiration for this snappy quilt of red, white, and blue.
Star blocks alternate with chain blocks that crisscross the quilt top.
Rotary cutting and strip piecing make this patriotic quilt easy to assemble.

Finished size of quilt: 83½" x 103½"   **Finished size of blocks:** 10" square

MATERIALS
4¾ yards of white fabric for blocks

4 yards of red fabric for star blocks
    and outer borders

2½ yards of blue fabric for chain
    blocks, inner border, corner
    squares, and binding

7½ yards of backing fabric or
    3⅛ yards of 90"-wide muslin

90" x 108" (queen-size) precut batting

Rotary cutter, acrylic ruler, and
    cutting mat

Template plastic (optional)

CUTTING
Refer to block diagrams to identify
each piece by letter. Instructions are
given for rotary cutting and strip piecing. If you prefer traditional cutting
and piecing methods, make templates
for patterns A–G on pages 136 and
137 and cut pieces for chain blocks
from strips listed for strip piecing.

From white fabric, cut:
❤ 6 (6¼"-wide) strips.
    From these, cut 32 (6¼") squares.
    Cut each square diagonally in both
    directions to get 128 C triangles.
❤ 10 (3"-wide) strips.
    From these, cut 128 (3") D
    squares.
❤ 9 (5½"-wide) strips.
    From these, cut 124 (3" x 5½")
    G rectangles.
❤ 17 (1¾"-wide) strips for strip sets
    X and Z.
❤ 3 (3"-wide) strips for Strip Set Y.

From red fabric, cut:
❤ 9 (6"-wide) strips for outer borders.
❤ 5 (5½"-wide) strips.
    From these, cut 32 (5½") A
    squares.
❤ 11 (3⅜"-wide) strips.
    From these, cut 128 (3⅜")
    squares. Cut each square in half
    diagonally to get 256 B triangles.

From blue fabric, cut:
❤ 9 (2"-wide) strips for binding.
❤ 9 (1¾"-wide) strips for inner
    borders.
❤ 17 (1¾"-wide) strips for strip sets
    X and Y.
❤ 3 (3"-wide) strips for Strip Set Z.
❤ 4 (6") squares for border corners.

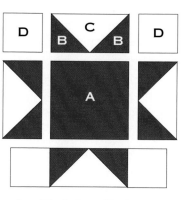

Star Block Assembly Diagram

MAKING STAR BLOCKS
1. Referring to *Star Block Assembly
Diagram,* arrange pieces for 1 block in
horizontal rows.
2. Join B triangles to short legs of
each C triangle as shown. Press seam
allowances toward B triangles.
3. Join 1 D square to each side of a
B-C unit to make top row of block.
Press seam allowances toward D
squares. Repeat to make bottom row.
4. For center row, join remaining B-
C units to opposite sides of A square.
Press seam allowances toward A
square.
5. Join rows to assemble block. Press
seam allowances toward outer rows.
6. Make 32 star blocks.

QUICK PIECING CHAIN BLOCKS

Note: If using blue striped fabric as in quilt shown, pay careful attention to direction of stripe when joining quick-cut segments to make units and blocks.

1. Referring to *strip set diagrams,* join designated strips as shown. Make 11 of Strip Set X, 3 of Strip Set Y, and 3 of Strip Set Z. Press all seam allowances toward blue fabric.

Strip Set X—Make 11.

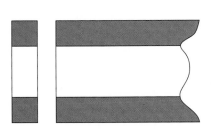

Strip Set Y—Make 3.

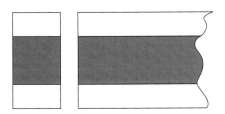

Strip Set Z—Make 3.

2. Cut 248 (1¾"-wide) segments from Strip Set X. Referring to *Four-Patch Diagram,* join segment pairs to make 1 four-patch. Make 124 four-patch units.

Four-Patch Diagram

3. Referring to *Chain Block Assembly Diagram,* join a four-patch to each side of 1 G rectangle to make top row of block. Repeat for bottom row.

4. Cut 62 (1¾"-wide) segments from Strip Set Y and 31 (3"-wide) segments from Strip Set Z.

5. To make center row of block, join a Y segment to each side of 1 Z segment as shown. Join a G rectangle to each end to complete center row.

6. Join rows. Make 31 chain blocks.

(continued)

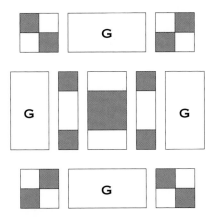

Chain Block Assembly Diagram

Designed and made by Liz Porter and Marianne Fons, 1993. Machine-quilted by Fern Stewart.

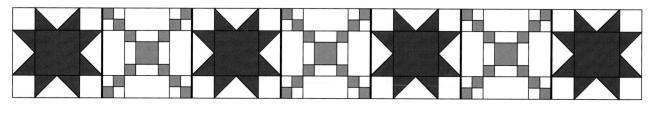

Row 1 Assembly Diagram

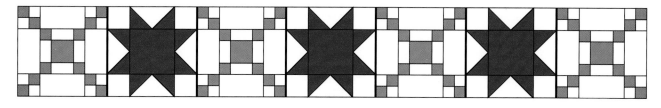

Row 2 Assembly Diagram

QUILT ASSEMBLY

1. Referring to *Row 1 Assembly Diagram,* join 4 star blocks and 3 chain blocks. Make 5 of Row 1.

2. Referring to *Row 2 Assembly Diagram,* join 4 chain blocks and 3 star blocks. Make 4 of Row 2.

3. Join rows, alternating rows 1 and 2.

4. Cut 1 blue border strip in half. For each side border, join 2½ strips.

5. Measure length of quilt top, measuring through middle rather than at edges. Trim borders to this length (approximately 90½"). Join borders to quilt sides, easing as necessary.

6. For each remaining border, join 2 strips end-to-end. Measure quilt width through middle of quilt top. Trim borders to this length (approximately 73"). Join borders to top and bottom edges of quilt.

7. Join red strips to prepare 4 outer borders in same manner as blue border. Before sewing borders to quilt, trim short borders to match width of quilt and long borders to match length. Join corner squares to ends of each short border.

8. Join long borders to quilt sides; then add remaining borders to top and bottom edges.

QUILTING AND FINISHING

1. Divide backing fabric into 3 (2½-yard) lengths. Join pieces, matching long edges.

2. Layer backing, batting, and quilt top; baste. (Backing seams will parallel top and bottom quilt edges.)

3. Quilt as desired. On the quilt shown, star blocks are outline-quilted and a diagonal square is quilted in center of block. Chain blocks are quilted as shown in *Chain Block Quilting Diagram.*

4. See General Instructions (page 174) for directions on making and applying binding. Make 390" of straight-grain binding.

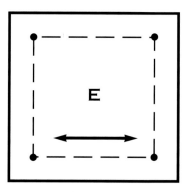

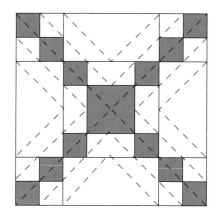

Chain Block Quilting Diagram

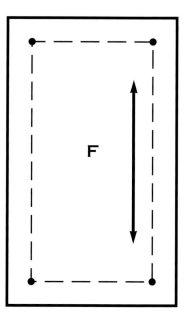

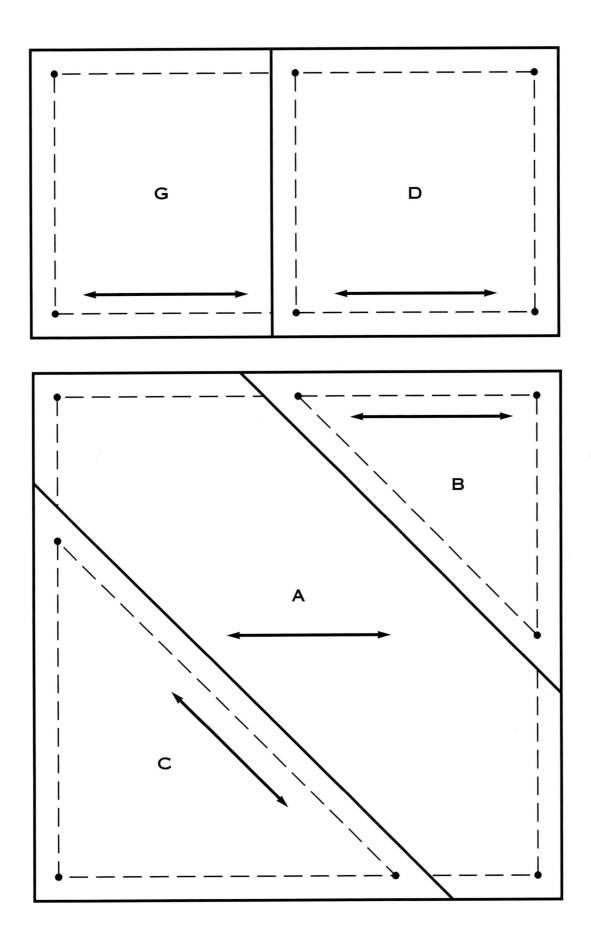

SCHOOL DAYS

Pinwheels and sashing accent 20 Schoolhouse blocks in this quilt, bordered by a caravan of 34 bus blocks. The group that made the blocks added personalized embroidery and appliqué details. To simplify construction of this quilt, instructions concentrate on rotary cutting and quick piecing.

Finished size of quilt: 84" x 93"

Finished size of Schoolhouse block: 9" square　　**Finished size of Schoolbus block:** 4½" x 9"

MATERIALS

4 yards of navy print fabric for borders, sashing, and pinwheels
1¾ yards of medium blue fabric for block backgrounds
1¾ yards of light blue fabric for block borders
1 yard of yellow fabric for buses
¾ yard of gold print fabric for inner border and pinwheels
⅜ yard of ivory fabric for bus windows
¼ yard of black fabric for bus wheels
¼ yard of red fabric for pinwheels
¼ yard of red solid fabric for apples
⅛ yard of green fabric for leaves
6" x 14" piece *each* of 20 blue fabrics for Schoolhouses
Scraps of 10 blue fabrics for roofs
½ yard of navy binding fabric
2¾ yards of 90"-wide muslin backing
90" x 108" (queen-size) precut batting
Rotary cutter, acrylic ruler, and cutting mat
Template plastic

CUTTING

Cutting instructions are for rotary cutting, except for appliqués and roof section of Schoolhouse block. Make templates for patterns on pages 142 and 143. Refer to diagrams on pages 140 and 142 to identify patchwork pieces. Patterns are not given for appliquéd and embroidered details such as people and flowers.

There are many pieces in this quilt, so it's a good idea to store cut pieces in labeled zip-top bags. You may prefer to cut pieces for each block as you work. We recommend that you cut borders first; then proceed to cut smaller pieces. Use scraps for small appliqués and pieces such as windows and doors.

Cut all strips crossgrain except for borders as noted.

From light blue fabric, cut:

- 5 (9½"-wide) strips.
  From these, cut 80 (2½" x 9½") strips for block borders.

From yellow fabric, cut:

- 6 (1"-wide) strips.
  From these, cut 34 (1" x 6¾") P rectangles.
- 7 (2"-wide) strips.
  From these, cut 34 (2" x 7¾") R rectangles.
- 6 (1⅛"-wide) strips for bus strip sets.

From navy print fabric, cut:

- 4 (2" x 95") lengthwise strips for outer border.
- 2 (5½" x 95") and 2 (2½" x 95") lengthwise strips for middle border.
- 4 (1½" x 74") lengthwise strips for first inner border.
- 3 (2½" x 74") lengthwise strips for vertical sashing.
- 1 (13½"-wide) strip.
  From this, cut 16 (2½" x 13½") strips for horizontal sashing.
- 8 (1⅞"-wide) strips.
  From these, cut 160 (1⅞") squares. Cut each square in half diagonally to get 320 pinwheel triangles.

From medium blue fabric, cut:

- 8 (2"-wide) strips.
  From these, cut 40 (2") N squares, 20 (2" x 6½") O rectangles, 34 (2" x 2¼") Q rectangles, and 34 (1¼" x 2") S rectangles.
- 2 (3½"-wide) strips.
  From these, cut 34 (1½" x 3½") T rectangles.
- 2 (9½"-wide) strips.
  From these, cut 68 (1¼" x 9½") U rectangles.
- 4 (5") squares for apple blocks.
- 20 *each* of Pattern M and M reversed.

From ivory fabric, cut:

- 5 (1¾"-wide) strips for bus strip sets.　　*(continued)*

Designed by Kansas quilter Jan Keeler and made by the staff and friends of Buckner Elementary School for retiring teacher Caroline Overton of Buckner, Missouri, 1988.

From gold print fabric, cut:

- ♥ 8 (1½"-wide) strips for second inner border.
- ♥ 4 (1⅞"-wide) strips.
  From these, cut 80 (1⅞") squares. Cut each square in half diagonally to get 160 pinwheel triangles.

From black fabric, cut:

- ♥ 68 wheels.
  Note: If desired, you can substitute 1½"-diameter buttons for wheels.

From red fabric, cut:

- ♥ 4 (1⅞"-wide) strips.
  From these, cut 80 (1⅞") squares. Cut each square in half diagonally to get 160 pinwheel triangles.

From red solid fabric, cut:

- ♥ 4 apples.

From green fabric, cut:

- ♥ 2 leaves and 2 leaves reversed.

From *each* fabric for houses, cut:

- ♥ 2 (1¼" x 3¾") B rectangles.
- ♥ 1 (1¾" x 3½") C rectangle.
- ♥ 1 (1" x 2¾") F rectangle.
- ♥ 1 (1¾" x 3½") G rectangle.
- ♥ 2 (1¾" x 4") H rectangles.
- ♥ 1 (1" x 6") I rectangle.
- ♥ 1 of Pattern J.

From *each* roof fabric, cut:

- ♥ 2 of Pattern L.
- ♥ 2 belfries.

From assorted scraps, cut:

- ♥ 20 bells.
- ♥ 20 (2" x 3¾") A rectangles for doors.
- ♥ 40 (1¾" x 2¾") E rectangles for windows.
- ♥ 1 (1" x 5") D rectangle, 1 (1" x 6") I rectangle, and 1 of Pattern K for each Schoolhouse.

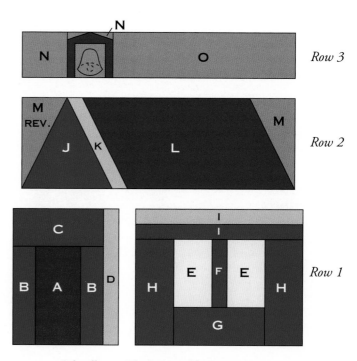

Schoolhouse Block Assembly Diagram

MAKING SCHOOLHOUSE BLOCKS

Refer to *Schoolhouse Block Assembly Diagram* to arrange pieces for each block. Pieces are joined in alphabetical order. Press seam allowances toward darker fabrics throughout.

1. For door section, join B pieces to sides of A rectangle; then sew C piece across top of door unit. Add D piece to right edge to complete section.

2. To begin main house section, join E window piece to sides of F rectangle; then sew G piece across bottom of window unit. Add H rectangles to both sides of unit as shown. Add contrasting I pieces as shown.

3. Join main house section to door section to complete Row 1 of block.

4. To make Row 2, join pieces J, K, L, M, and M reversed as shown.

5. To prepare belfry for appliqué, turn under edges at top and interior, leaving bottom and sides unturned. Align unturned edges of belfry with edges of 1 N square and pin in place. Appliqué belfry to N square.

6. Appliqué bell in center of belfry. Add embroidery details as shown on bell pattern.

7. To make Row 3, sew remaining N square and O rectangle to sides of appliquéd N square as shown.

8. Join rows 1, 2, and 3.

9. Make 20 blocks. Add appliquéd or embroidered details as desired.

MAKING PINWHEELS

Quilt shown has an unequal number of gold and red pinwheels. For balance and ease of construction, these instructions call for an equal number.

1. Referring to *Pinwheel Assembly Diagram,* join a navy triangle to each gold and red triangle to make 160 triangle-squares of *each* color combination. Press seam allowances toward navy fabric.

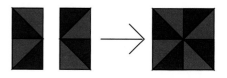

Pinwheel Assembly Diagram

2. Join triangle-squares in pairs and then in sets of 4 as shown to make 40 navy/red pinwheels. In same manner, make 40 navy/gold pinwheels.

ADDING BLOCK BORDERS

Press seam allowances toward sashing strips throughout.

1. Referring to *Block Border Diagram,* sew light blue border strips to sides of each Schoolhouse block.

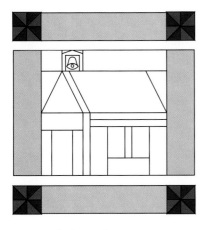

Block Border Diagram

2. Sew matching pinwheels to ends of 2 more border strips. Join these strips to top and bottom of block.

3. Add borders and pinwheels to all 20 Schoolhouse blocks, using navy/red pinwheels on 10 blocks and navy/gold pinwheels on 10 blocks.

INNER QUILT ASSEMBLY

Press seam allowances toward sashing and/or borders throughout.

1. Starting with a red pinwheel block, join 5 bordered blocks and 4 navy horizontal sashing strips to make a vertical row as shown at left of *Row Assembly Diagram.* Note pinwheel colors alternating down the row.

2. Starting with a gold pinwheel block, make second row in same manner.

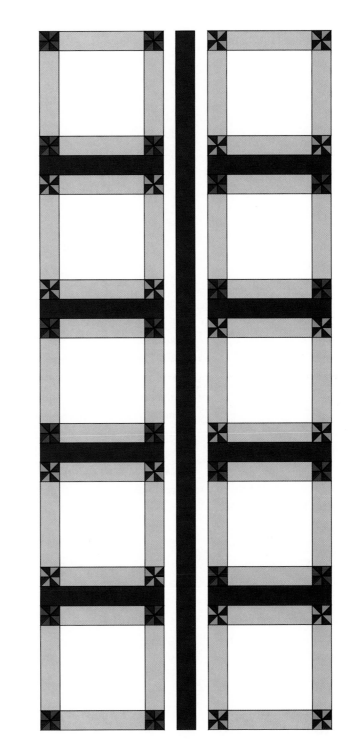

Row Assembly Diagram

3. Repeat steps 1 and 2 to make 2 more rows.

4. Join block rows, sewing a vertical sashing strip between rows. Ease rows as needed to fit sashing strip.

5. Sew a navy inner border strip to both quilt sides.

6. Measure width of quilt, measuring through middle rather than at edges. Trim 2 remaining navy inner border strips to this length (approximately 60½"). Join these to top and bottom of quilt, easing as necessary.

(continued)

7. For gold inner border, join pairs of gold strips end-to-end to make 4 border strips. Measure quilt length and trim 2 strips to this length (approximately 75½"); then sew these to quilt sides. Measure quilt width as before and trim 2 remaining borders to match (approximately 62½"). Sew these to top and bottom of quilt.

8. Referring to quilt photograph, add 5½"-wide navy borders to quilt sides in same manner. Join 2½"-wide strips to top and bottom edges to complete middle border.

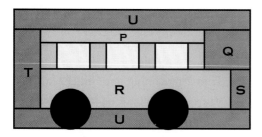

Schoolbus Strip Set Diagram

MAKING SCHOOLBUS BORDER

1. Referring to *Schoolbus Strip Set Diagram,* join strips as shown to make 1 strip set. Cut remaining strips in half to make a half strip set. Press seam allowances toward yellow fabric. From these strip sets, cut 34 (1½"-wide) segments for bus windows.

2. Referring to *Schoolbus Block Diagram,* sew a yellow P rectangle to 1 long edge of each window segment. Sew a blue Q square to right side of unit to complete top section of bus.

Schoolbus Block Diagram

3. For bottom section of bus, join a blue S rectangle to short side of each yellow R rectangle.

4. Join bottom section of bus to top section.

5. Sew a blue T rectangle to left side of each bus. Press seam allowances toward T piece. Then sew blue U rectangles to top and bottom of each block.

6. Appliqué 2 wheels to each bus.

7. Make 34 Schoolbus blocks. Add details to buses and wheels as desired.

8. For apple blocks, appliqué 1 leaf and 1 apple to each blue background square. Embroider stem and leaf veins as desired.

9. For each side border, join 9 blocks in a row. Referring to photograph, sew these to sides of quilt, easing as necessary. For top and bottom borders, make 2 rows of 8 blocks each, sewing an apple block to both ends of each row. Sew these borders to top and bottom edges of quilt.

10. Measure quilt length as before. Trim 2 (2"-wide) navy outer borders to this length (approximately 90½") and sew these to quilt sides. Measure width of quilt and trim remaining outer borders to this length (approximately 81½"). Join these to top and bottom of quilt.

QUILTING AND FINISHING

1. Layer backing, batting, and quilt top; baste.

2. Mark desired quilting designs on quilt top. Quilt shown is quilted in-the-ditch, with perpendicular lines quilted through wide middle borders. An ABC motif is quilted in block borders.

3. Quilt as desired.

4. See General Instructions (page 174) for directions on making and applying binding. Make 360" of straight-grain binding.

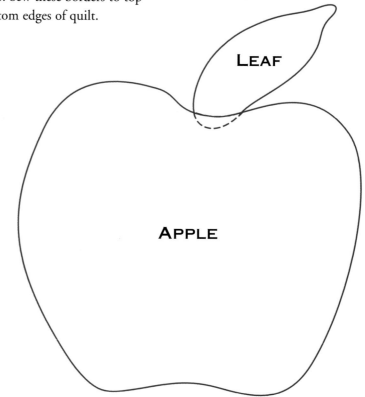

LEAF

APPLE

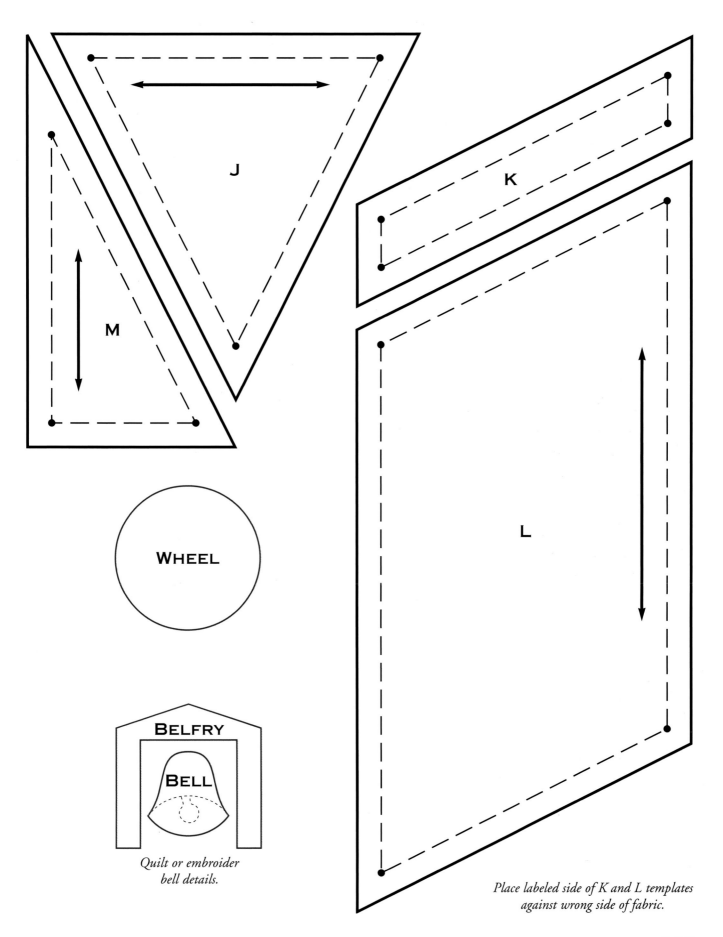

J

M

K

L

WHEEL

BELFRY

BELL

*Quilt or embroider
bell details.*

*Place labeled side of K and L templates
against wrong side of fabric.*

143

AUTUMN APPLES

Iowa quilter Cheryl Mathre used quick piecing methods to make a veritable orchard of 18 apple blocks. Surrounded by setting triangles quilted with more apples, this wall hanging is an excellent project on which to learn strip piecing and diagonal-corner techniques. You'll find patterns for traditional cutting and piecing, too.

Finished size of quilt: 36⅞" x 47½"   **Finished size of block:** 5½" square

MATERIALS

1½ yards of dark red print fabric for borders, patchwork, and binding
1¼ yards of cream fabric
1 yard of light red print fabric for setting triangles and patchwork
⅛ yard of green fabric for leaves
1½ yards of backing fabric
45" x 60" (crib-size) precut batting
Rotary cutter, acrylic ruler, and cutting mat
Template plastic (optional)

CUTTING

Before cutting, choose a piecing technique. We recommend strip piecing to make nine-patches and the diagonal-corner method to round out the blocks. (See pages 164 and 165 for directions on these techniques.) Cutting and piecing instructions are given for these methods.

For traditional cutting, make templates for patterns A–F on page 147. Refer to *Traditional Piecing Diagram* to identify pieces by letter and to assemble blocks.

From dark red print fabric, cut:

❤ 5 (2"-wide) strips for binding.
❤ 4 (3"-wide) border strips.
❤ 4 (1½"-wide) strips for strip sets.
❤ 2 (2½"-wide) strips.
  From these, cut 18 (2½" x 3½") C rectangles.
❤ 3 (1"-wide) strips.
  From these, cut 18 (1" x 6") E rectangles.
❤ 1 (6¼"-wide) strip.
  From this, cut 2 (6¼") squares. Cut each square in half diagonally to get 4 corner setting triangles.

From light red print fabric, cut:

❤ 1 (11⅞"-wide) strip.
  From this, cut 3 (11⅞") squares. Cut each square in half diagonally in both directions to get 10 setting triangles and 2 extra.
❤ 4 (1½"-wide) strips for strip sets.
❤ 2 (2½"-wide) strips.
  From these, cut 18 (2½" x 3½") C rectangles.
❤ 3 (1"-wide) strips.
  From these, cut 18 (1" x 5½") E rectangles.

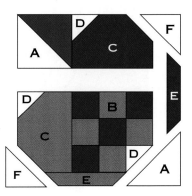

Traditional Piecing Diagram

From cream fabric, cut:

❤ 1 (2⅞"-wide) strip.
  From this, cut 9 (2⅞") squares. Cut each square in half diagonally to get 18 A triangles for leaves.
❤ 2 (2½"-wide) strips.
  From these, cut 18 (2½") squares for A diagonal corners.
❤ 1 (1½"-wide) strip for Strip Set 3.
❤ 2 (1½"-wide) strips.
  From these, cut 36 (1½") squares for D diagonal corners.
❤ 2 (2"-wide) strips.
  From these, cut 36 (2") squares for F diagonal corners.
❤ 14 (1½"-wide) strips.
  From these, cut 36 (1½" x 6") pieces and 36 (1½" x 8") pieces for framing strips.

From green fabric, cut:

❤ 1 (2⅞"-wide) strip.
  From this, cut 9 (2⅞") squares. Cut each square in half diagonally to get 18 A triangles for leaves.

PIECING BLOCKS

1. Referring to *Traditional Piecing Diagram,* join green and cream A triangles to make leaf squares. Make 18 leaf squares.

2. Referring to *strip set diagrams,* make 1 of each strip set. Press all seam allowances toward light red fabric. Cut 18 (1½"-wide) segments from *each* strip set.

Strip Set 1 Diagram

Strip Set 2 Diagram

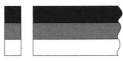

Strip Set 3 Diagram

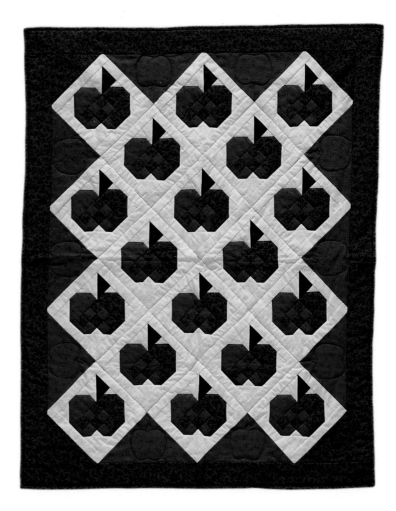

Designed and made by Cheryl Mathre of Des Moines, Iowa, 1994.

MAKING A HANGING SLEEVE

Wall quilts and large quilts that are hung for display often have a sleeve on the back through which you can insert a pole for hanging.

1. From extra backing fabric or muslin, cut an 8½"-wide strip that measures the width of the quilt. Piece short pieces as needed to achieve length.

2. On both ends of strip, turn 1" to wrong side twice and hem. With wrong sides facing, join long edges. Press seam allowances open, centering the seam on one side of the tube.

3. With seam allowance against quilt back, place sleeve just below binding at top of quilt, centering it between quilt sides. Blindstitch top and bottom edges of sleeve to backing only, making sure no stitches go through to quilt top *(see diagram).*

Back of quilt

Sleeve

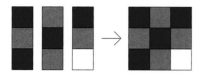

Nine-Patch Diagram—Make 18.

3. Select 1 segment from each strip set. Arranging segments as shown in *Nine-Patch Diagram,* join segments to make 1 nine-patch. Make 18 nine-patch units.

4. Referring to *Diagonal Corner Diagram,* join cream D squares to all C rectangles. Light and dark units are stitched differently, so be sure to position corners and sew in diagonal direction shown. Make 18 C-D units of each fabric.

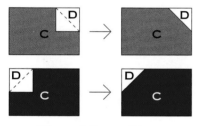

Diagonal Corner Diagram

5. Referring to *Block Assembly Diagram,* sew a light red C-D unit to left side of all nine-patch units. Position nine-patch as shown, with cream square at lower right corner. Press seam allowances toward C-D unit.

6. Join a leaf square to end of all dark red C-D units, positioning units as shown. Press seam allowances toward leaf square.

7. Join units from steps 5 and 6 as shown. Press seam allowances away from nine-patch.

8. Referring to *Block Assembly Diagram,* join a light red E strip to bottom of each block. Press seam allowance toward E rectangle; then add a dark red E rectangle to adjacent side as shown.

9. Referring to *Block Assembly Diagram,* position F diagonal-corner squares at top right and bottom left corners of each block and A diagonal-corner square at bottom right. Stitch in diagonal directions indicated. In this manner, complete 18 blocks.

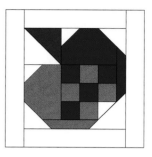

Block Framing Diagram

FRAMING BLOCKS

1. Referring to *Block Framing Diagram,* sew 6"-long framing strips to top and bottom edges of all blocks. Press seam allowances toward framing strips.

2. Add 8"-long framing strips to block sides. Press seam allowances toward framing strips. Framed blocks should be 8" square, including seam allowances.

QUILT ASSEMBLY

1. Referring to photograph, join framed blocks, setting triangles, and corner triangles in diagonal rows. Press seam allowances in alternate directions

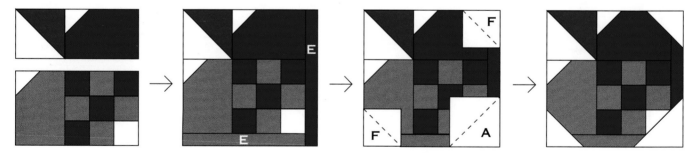

Block Assembly Diagram

from row to row. Join rows to assemble quilt top.

2. Measure length of quilt through middle rather than at edges and trim 2 border strips to this length (approximately 42⅜"). Sew these borders to quilt sides. Press seam allowances toward borders.

3. Measure width of quilt through middle, including side borders. Trim remaining borders to this length (approximately 37⅜"). Sew borders to top and bottom edges of quilt. Press seam allowances toward borders.

QUILTING AND FINISHING

1. Mark desired quilting designs on quilt top. A pattern for apple quilting motif used in setting triangles is on this page.

2. Layer backing, batting, and quilt top; baste.

3. Quilt marked design. Quilt in-the-ditch along seams joining blocks. Add additional quilting as desired.

4. See General Instructions (page 174) for directions on making and applying binding. Make 185" of straight-grain binding.

Apple Quilting Design

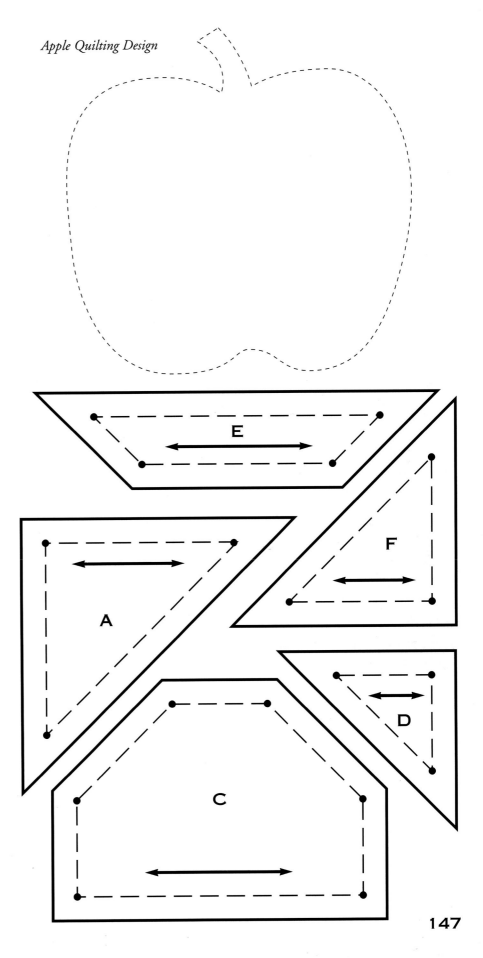

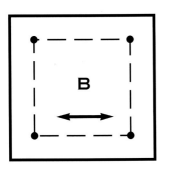

FOLK ART STOCKINGS

Decorative buttonhole stitching defines the primitive-style designs on these festive stockings.
The pleasure of using wool for appliqué is that raw edges do not have to be turned. For her appliqués, folk artist
Jackie Leckband finds closely woven wool flannel or recycles cuttings from old clothes.

Finished size of stocking: 9" x 20"

Designed and made by Jackie Leckband of Earlham, Iowa, 1994.

MATERIALS

⅓ yard of coat-weight wool for each stocking

Scraps of colored wool for appliqués

2 (½"-diameter) buttons for hanging loop

Embroidery floss or size 5 pearl cotton

Large-eyed, sharp needles

Freezer paper

CUTTING

1. For a master pattern, cut a 12" x 22" piece of freezer paper. Trace stocking foot from patterns on pages 150 and 151, joining sections at dots as indicated. Referring to diagram shown on pattern, extend lines to complete stocking leg on master pattern. Do not to add seam allowances.

2. Pin pattern to wool fabric. Cut 1 stocking front; then reverse pattern to cut 1 stocking back.

3. From appliqué patterns on pages 149–152, trace desired designs onto freezer paper. Cut out paper patterns, including 1 for hanging loop. If desired, make patterns for optional toe and heel.

4. Pin patterns to wool scraps. Cut out shapes on pattern lines, without adding seam allowances.

5. If desired, cut a contrasting band for top edge of stocking. Cut a band 1½"–2½" wide. Bottom edge of band can be straight, scalloped, or curved.

ASSEMBLY

1. For contrasting toe and heel, pin shapes in place, aligning outer edges with edge of stocking. Buttonhole-stitch around interior edges only, since outer edges will be covered when stocking front is joined to back.

2. Pin appliqués to stocking front as

148

desired. Use contrasting pearl cotton or floss to buttonhole-stitch appliqués in place. (See page 167 of General Instructions for tips on buttonhole stitch.) Note special instructions on some appliqué patterns.

3. Position decorative band at top edge of stocking front and embellish as desired.

4. With wrong sides facing, align edges of stocking front and back. Leaving top open, buttonhole-stitch edges together through both layers.

5. Buttonhole-stitch edges of hanging loop strip. Fold strip in half and position ends at top right corner edge of stocking front. Place a button on top of loop ends and a matching button in same position on stocking back. Hand-sew through both buttons to secure loop.

No buttonhole stitching.

Use buttonhole stitch for outer edges of all appliqués except as noted.

Black lines on appliqué patterns indicate optional decorative stitching.

For window and door inserts, cut a piece of wool slightly larger than opening. Slip wool under cut-out area before stitching house edges.

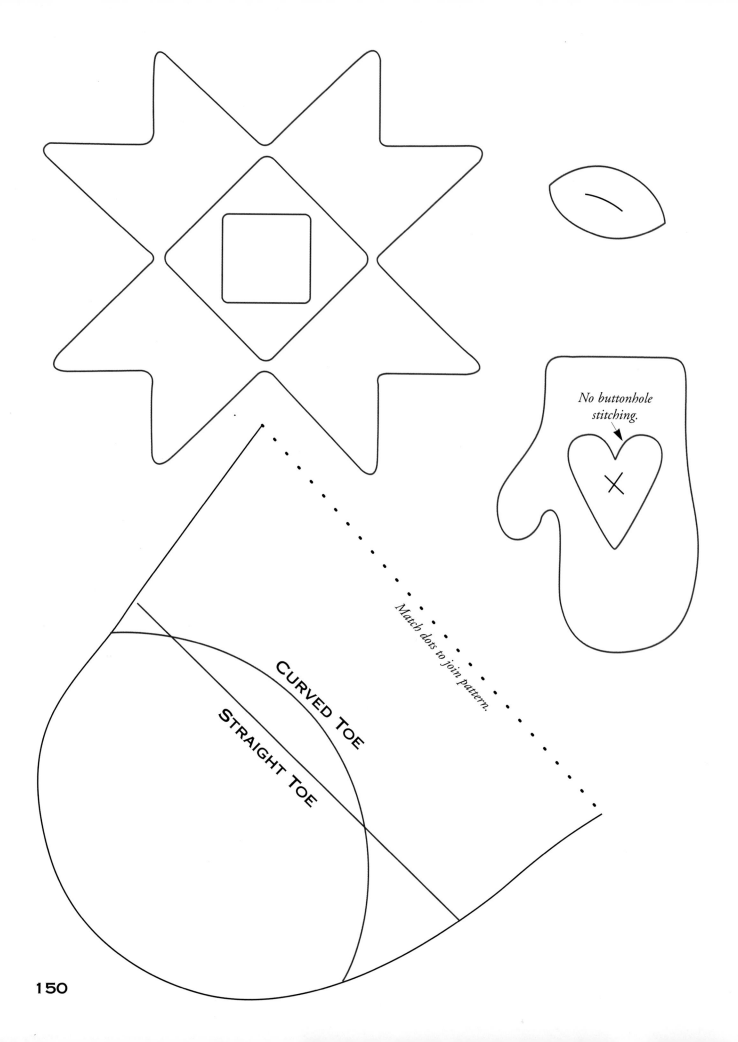

No buttonhole
stitching.

Match dots to join pattern.

CURVED TOE

STRAIGHT TOE

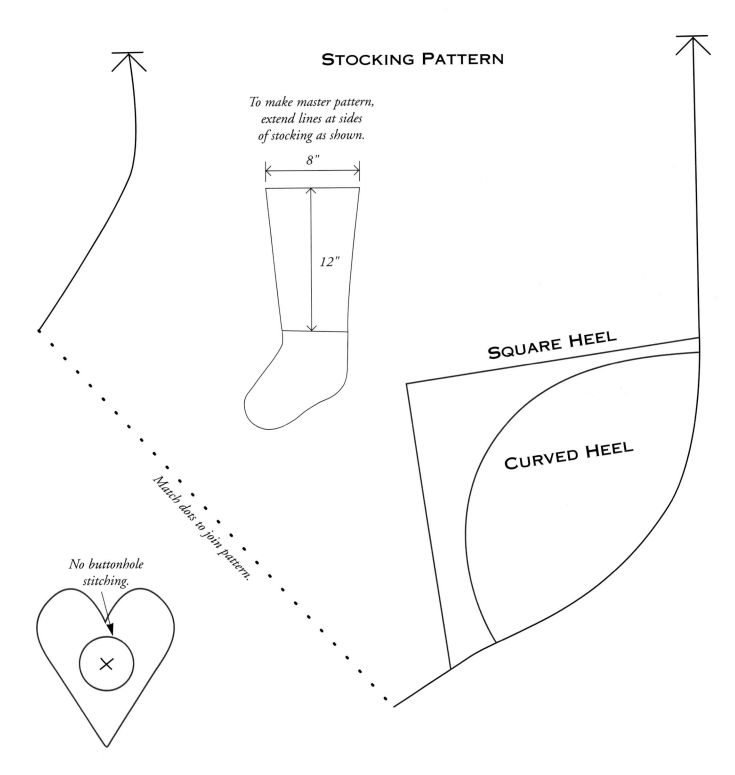

HANGING LOOP

STOCKING PATTERN

To make master pattern, extend lines at sides of stocking as shown.

8"

12"

Match dots to join pattern.

SQUARE HEEL

CURVED HEEL

No buttonhole stitching.

151

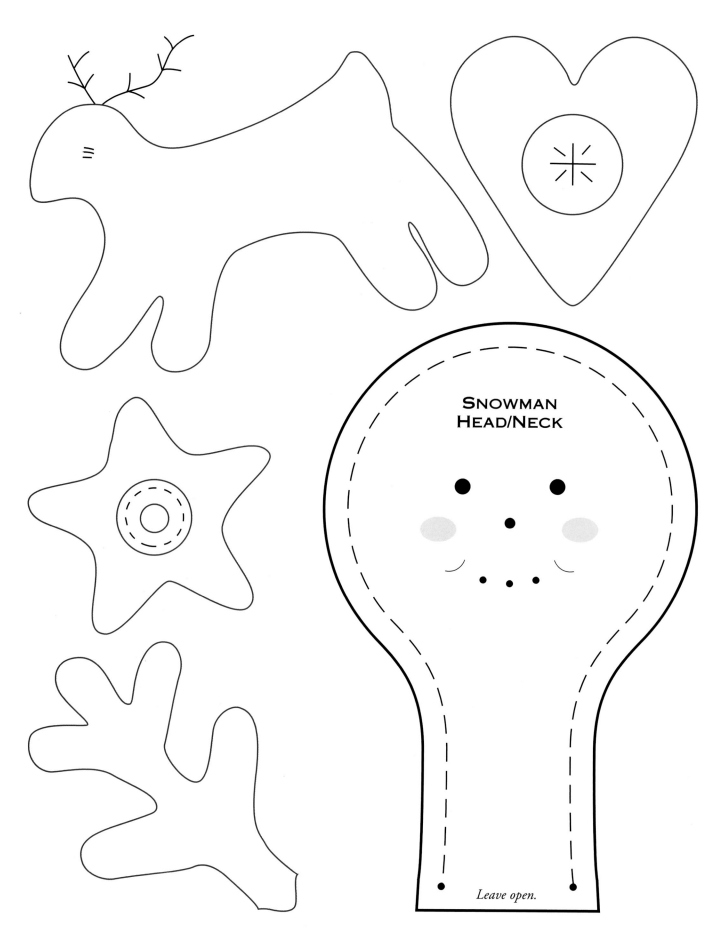

SNOWMAN
HEAD/NECK

Leave open.

SNOWMAN

*Banish winter blues with this cheerful snowman doll. His body is a circle of flannel,
loosely stuffed and gathered around a simple head/neck piece. Dress him up with scarf and mittens made
from fabric scraps and add a stocking cap of ribbing. Draw his facial features with marker and crayon.*

Finished size: Approximately 7" tall

MATERIALS

½ yard of white cotton flannel

4" x 6" piece of cotton ribbing
for hat

1½" x 18" strip of striped fabric
for scarf

3" square of striped fabric
for mittens

Permanent black marker and
red crayon

Polyester stuffing

½ cup of rice or popcorn kernels
for filling

White quilting thread

Template plastic

CUTTING

Make templates for head/neck and
mitten patterns.

From white flannel, cut:

❤ 1 (14"-diameter) circle for body.

❤ 2 head/neck pieces.

From red striped fabric, cut:

❤ 1 mitten and 1 mitten reversed.

*Designed and made by
Liz Porter, 1994.*

ASSEMBLY

1. With right sides facing and raw
edges aligned, sew around head/neck
pieces, leaving bottom of neck open.
Clip seam and turn right side out.
Stuff head firmly. Hand-sew neck
bottom closed.

2. Using quilting thread, make run-
ning stitches around perimeter of
flannel circle, ¼" inside raw edge. Do
not clip thread; leave needle threaded.

3. Draw up gathering thread slightly
to cup edge of flannel circle. Place
rice (or popcorn) and a large handful
of stuffing in circle center.

4. Position head/neck in circle center. Pull gathers up tightly around
neck bottom. Using gathering thread,
tack gathered edge of circle to neck.
Secure thread.

5. Hand-sew right and left mittens
to body front.

6. To fringe short ends of scarf,
make 3 (1½"-deep) cuts in each end.
Trim fringe at an angle. Tie scarf
around neck, concealing top of gathered flannel circle.

7. Use black marker to draw eyes,
nose, and mouth on face as shown on
head/neck pattern. Lightly rub red
crayon on cheeks.

8. For hat, bring 4"-long sides of
ribbing together and stitch. Finger-
press seam allowances open. With
seam centered on 1 side, stitch across
1 open edge. Turn right side out.

9. Fold up ¼" on bottom of hat;
then fold up another ¼" so raw edge
of ribbing is concealed. Tack cuff to
secure. Place hat on head.

ADVENT CALENDAR

Make 24 miniature quilt blocks to count the days of December, adding one block to the calendar each day until Christmas Eve. Select patterns from the Bonus 3" Blocks section (page 78). Fabric corners hold each quilted block in place on the background quilt.

Finished size of quilt: 24¼" x 35¾"   **Finished size of blocks:** 3" square

Designed and made by Mary Ellen Egbert of Sydney, Ohio, 1991.

MATERIALS

1¾ yards of cream solid fabric for block backgrounds, windows, and backing

1½ yards of floral print fabric for corner pockets, sashing squares, and binding

¾ yard *each* of red and green solid fabrics for sashing

Assorted fabric scraps for blocks

1 yard of 45"-wide polyester fleece

Rotary cutter, acrylic ruler, and cutting mat

35 (⅛"-diameter) gold beads

CUTTING

Follow instructions below to cut pieces for wall hanging and block backing. Add remaining fabrics to scraps for sampler blocks. To cut pieces for blocks, see instructions for Bonus 3" Blocks section (page 78).

From red solid fabric, cut:
❤ 16 (⅞"-wide) strips for sashing strip sets.

From green solid fabric, cut:
❤ 8 (⅞"-wide) strips for sashing strip sets.

From cream fabric, cut:
❤ 3 (5"-wide) strips.
  From these, cut 24 (5") squares for windows.
❤ 3 (4"-wide) strips.
  From these, cut 24 (4") squares for block backings.
❤ 1 (26" x 38") piece for wall hanging back.

From floral print, cut:
❤ 5 (2"-wide) strips.
  From these, cut 96 (2") squares for corner pockets.
❤ 2 (1⅝"-wide) strips.
  From these, cut 35 (1⅝") sashing squares.
❤ 15 (2"-wide) strips for binding.

From fleece, cut:
❤ 1 (26" x 38") piece for wall hanging.
❤ 24 (4") squares for blocks.

MAKING WALL HANGING

1. Referring to *Sashing Strip Set Diagram,* join red and green strips as shown to make 8 strip sets. Press seam allowances toward red strips. From these strip sets, cut 58 (5"-wide) segments for sashing.

Sashing Strip Set Diagram—Make 8.

2. With wrong sides facing, press each floral 2" square in half diagonally to make a triangle for corner pockets. Aligning raw edges, pin a pressed triangle to each corner of each 5" window square.

3. Referring to *Sashing Row Diagram,* join 5 sashing squares and 4 sashing strips. Make 7 sashing rows.

4. Referring to *Block Row Diagram,* join 5 sashing strips and 4 prepared window squares. Keep edges of corner pockets aligned with window squares as you stitch. Make 6 block rows. Press seam allowances toward sashing strips in all rows.

5. Join rows, alternating sashing rows and block rows.

6. Layer backing, fleece, and quilt top; baste. Quilt as desired.

7. Trim fleece and backing to ¼" beyond quilt edge. See General Instructions (page 174) for directions on making and applying binding. Use floral print strips to make 125" of straight-grain binding.

8. Sewing through all layers, sew a bead to center of each sashing square.

9. See page 145 for directions on making a hanging sleeve.

MAKING BLOCKS

1. To cut pieces for blocks, see instructions for Bonus 3" Blocks section (page 78). If you select appliqué blocks, appliqué pieces to 3½" background squares cut from remaining cream fabric. Since finished blocks will not be subjected to extensive use or repeated washing, you can make appliqué blocks quickly by fusing pieces in place.

2. Layer a fleece square and 4" backing square under each block. Quilt as desired.

3. Bind edges of each block with floral print strips as for wall hanging.

4. Insert bound blocks into wall hanging windows, tucking blocks under corner pockets.

Sashing Row Diagram—Make 7.

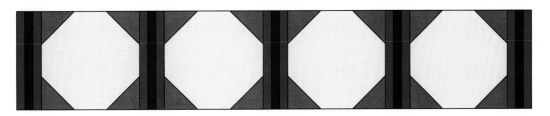

Block Row Diagram—Make 6.

GENERAL INSTRUCTIONS

BASIC TOOLS FOR YOUR SEWING BASKET

Quilters love to fill their sewing baskets with the latest gadgets and supplies. Quilt shops always seem to have new things, and it's fun to experiment with them all. We've limited this list, however, to those items we believe are basic for making the projects in this book. If you've already done a little quilting, you probably have most of them.

For specialized techniques, you may need additional items. We've listed these tools and supplies with the instructions for special techniques that are given throughout the book.

CUTTING TOOLS

Heavy-duty Rotary Cutter. Rotary cutters are available in a variety of sizes and shapes. Select the one that is most comfortable for you to use. Have plenty of *replacement blades* on hand.

Cutting Mat. An 18" x 24" mat, ruled with a grid of 1" or 2" squares, is adequate for most cutting. Smaller and larger sizes are available for specialized needs.

Rulers. Choose rulers that are marked in ⅛" increments and have guidelines for cutting 45° and 60° angles. We have found that there are three rulers we can't do without: a 6" x 24" ruler for cutting

strips across the fabric width; a 6" x 12" ruler for cutting segments from pieced strip sets; and a 15" square for straightening fabric ends before cutting strips, cutting background squares, checking blocks for size accuracy, or squaring off corners before sewing on binding.

Fabric Shears and Utility Scissors. Save your fabric shears for cutting fabric so they will remain sharp. Use utility scissors for cutting paper and template plastic.

SEWING SUPPLIES

Sewing Machine. A straight-stitch sewing machine is all you need for sewing patchwork. You may

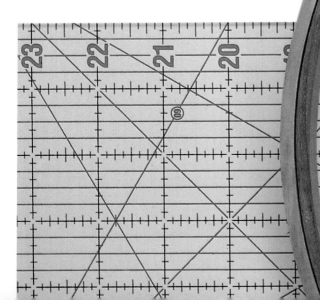

need a more versatile sewing machine if you want to do machine appliqué, machine embroidery, or machine quilting. A presser foot with ¼"-wide toes—*a patchwork foot*—is available for most machines. If you don't have this kind of foot, tape a guide on the throat plate as described under "Machine Patchwork Basics" (page 162). Keep the machine in good working order and replace needles (size 80/12) frequently. Have a *seam ripper* handy.

Sewing Thread. We like 100% cotton or cotton-covered polyester thread for machine patchwork. Medium gray is often the best color to use for sewing patchwork since it blends with most fabrics.

Straight Pins and Pin Holder. Choose long, thin, rustproof dressmaker's pins with small glass heads. We adore our magnetic pin holders, especially when we need to pick up pins that we have dropped.

Hand-Sewing Needles and Thimble. For hand patchwork and appliqué, use long, thin needles such as size 11 or 12 *sharps*. Choose a thimble that fits the middle finger of your sewing hand.

Iron and Ironing Board. You will need an iron with both steam and dry settings.

OTHER NOTIONS

Fabric Storage Containers. We like to store cut pieces, fabric scraps, and assorted sewing notions in *plastic bags* with zipper-type closures. Use a permanent marker to label bags. Large *pizza boxes* are good for storing and carrying completed blocks. (Ask for clean boxes at a local pizzeria.) Line the bottom of the box with a square of batting to keep the blocks from sliding around. Clear *plastic sweater boxes* are perfect containers for folded fabric pieces and strips. We also use them to store extra yardage, templates, and miscellaneous items for a specific project. This way, all the components stay together while we work on a quilt.

Pencils and Markers. A *mechanical pencil* that holds 0.5-mm (thin) lead is excellent for marking fabrics and drawing on paper. For marking quilt tops, you may also use a *chalk marker, washable graphite pencil,* or an *artist's silver drawing pencil* that shows up well on both light and dark fabrics and washes out easily. Keep pencils sharp so they make neat, thin lines. We do not recommend water-erasable or other "disappearing" felt-tip fabric markers. We know of many instances where the chemicals in the markers have stained, bleached, or otherwise damaged fabrics. Always test markers on fabric scraps before using them on your quilt.

Dressmaker's Measuring Tape. A standard 60"-long tape works fine, but we love our 120"-long measuring tapes, especially when measuring for borders.

Plastic-coated Freezer Paper. Quilters have found many uses for the plastic-coated freezer paper sold in grocery stores. We use it for disposable templates for both patchwork and appliqué and as a fabric stabilizer for some types of machine appliqué.

Template Plastic. Quilt shops and many fabric stores sell semi-transparent sheets of lightweight vinyl to use for templates. For some projects in this book, template material is listed as optional. Although we use template-free rotary cutting methods to cut most patchwork, we occasionally make plastic templates to mark and cut shapes in the traditional way.

QUILTING IMPLEMENTS

Quilt Hoop or Frame. For hand quilting, we recommend holding the basted layers of a quilt taut in a hoop or frame.

Quilting Thread. For hand quilting, choose quilting thread in colors that coordinate with the quilt fabrics. For machine quilting, use sewing thread or clear monofilament.

Quilting Needles. For hand quilting, use short, strong needles called "betweens." A size 8 between is recommended for beginners.

FABRICS FOR QUILTS

We use 100% cotton broadcloth-weight fabric for quilts. It's easy to sew, not too stretchy or too tightly woven. It doesn't ravel easily, it washes well, and it is relatively colorfast. Cotton also takes a crease well, so patchwork seams are easy to press and seam allowances stay put when folded under for appliqué.

CHOOSING FABRICS

Many quilters feel insecure about choosing fabrics, but don't be afraid to trust your instincts. Go with what you like. If you are making a quilt for someone else, perhaps that person can help you look for fabric.

When we shop for fabric, we put combinations of bolts together on a large table. Then we step back and look at the overall mix of values and visual textures. If one fabric looks out of place, we replace it with another. Sometimes we purchase just ¼ yard of each fabric to make a sample block and actually test our combination before buying all the fabric for a quilt. Warning—Some fabrics sell out quickly, so don't wait too long before going back to the shop to make your purchases.

Fabric companies create collections designed to work well together. This can make easy work of your shopping. For example, fabrics from one collection were used for *Snoozin' with Snakes*. We used our own signature line of fabrics for the *Basket* quilts and *Stars and Stripes Forever!*

If you need help making your selection, several resources are available. Employees of quilt shops and fabric stores are usually glad to assist. Some shops and mail-order sources offer sets of coordinating fabrics in ¼-yard or ½-yard cuts. Buying sets is an easy way to take the guesswork out of combining fabrics and to see how an experienced shop owner has combined fabrics.

Visit quilt shows to view the work of other quilters. Many shows allow you to photograph quilts on exhibit. Take notes on fabric and color combinations that you find exciting, inspiring, particularly successful, or that you feel would work well for a project you plan to make.

Another system for choosing colors relies on formal relationships such as monochromatic, analogous, and complementary. Quilt shops keep on hand several excellent books that explain the application of color theory in quiltmaking.

One simple approach to combining fabrics is to choose one fabric that has several colors and then select coordinating fabrics in colors contained in the theme fabric. Sometimes we don't even purchase the theme fabric—we just use it to inspire a great color combination.

Color is not the only factor to consider when combining fabrics. To increase the visual texture of your quilts, choose fabrics with small-, medium-, and large-scale prints. As you combine printed fabrics, choose those that have the same mood or degree of sophistication. Fabric printed with baby rattles and baby bottles will probably not work well with stylish tropical prints or with prints suitable for your husband or teenager.

In order for the design to "read" in your quilt, you need contrast in value—light, medium, and dark—so that some design elements advance or become predominant, and others recede and create the background.

PURCHASING FABRIC

The materials list with each project in this book gives the amount of each fabric needed. We always allow for extra fabric in our estimates, as much as ½ yard for the major fabrics in the quilt and ⅛–¼ yard for other fabrics. We don't mind having fabric left over to add to our scrap bags. It's also nice to know that we will have sufficient fabric to finish a project even if we make a minor cutting error.

PREPARING FABRIC

We recommend that you wash, dry, and press fabrics before using them in quilts. Washing preshrinks the fabric and removes sizing, chemical finishes, and excess dye. You can wash like colors with the family laundry. We prewash fabrics in warm water and detergent or Orvus Paste soap (available at quilt shops or livestock supply stores), dry them at a medium or permanent-press setting in the dryer, and then steam-iron as needed to remove wrinkles.

Some dark fabrics bleed or release dye during washing. To test a fabric for colorfastness, stop your washer during the final rinse. Scoop out some rinse water in a clear glass and look for color. If the fabric is still bleeding, wash it again. If it continues to release color, don't use it in your quilt, or use it only with fabrics of similar color.

CUTTING BASICS

We find that rotary-cut pieces are usually more accurate than those marked with templates and cut with scissors. Quick cutting, often combined with quick-piecing methods, helps us produce quilts just as beautiful as those made piece by piece, but in much less time. We use the time we save to make more quilts!

Most of the projects in this book can be rotary cut. However, full-size patterns are given for most projects in case you prefer traditional cutting and piecing methods. You can also use these patterns to check the accuracy of rotary-cut pieces. Even if you are quick cutting, some projects require a few templates for shapes that do not lend themselves to rotary cutting or for use as guides to mark matching points on set-in pieces.

Solid lines on the patterns indicate cut size; dashed lines indicate sewing lines and show the finished size of the piece. *Dimensions given for borders, strips, and rotary-cut pieces always include ¼" seam allowances.*

ROTARY CUTTING STRIPS AND BASIC PIECES

Rotary cutting usually begins with cutting strips that are then cut into smaller pieces. For the projects in this book, *cut all strips across the fabric width* (selvage to selvage), unless instructions state otherwise. The instructions in this book specify the width and number of strips to cut from each fabric as well as the number and size of the pieces to cut from each strip.

Squaring-up Fabric. Before you cut strips or other pieces, straighten one end of the fabric by trimming it as described here so that the cut edge is at a right angle to the selvages.

1. Begin by folding the fabric in half on the lengthwise grain, matching selvage edges *(Photo A)*. You may need to misalign the cut edges to get the selvages to line up; pressing out the center fold will make this easier.

2. Lay the folded fabric on a cutting mat with selvages nearest you; fold the fabric in half lengthwise again, bringing selvages to center fold. By folding the fabric in fourths in this manner, cuts will be a manageable 11" long.

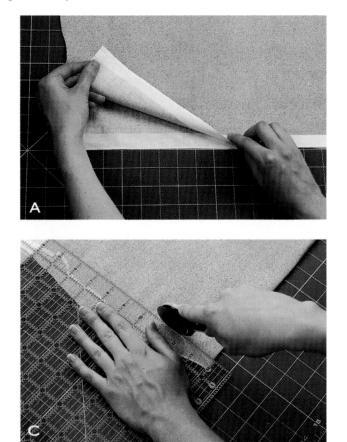

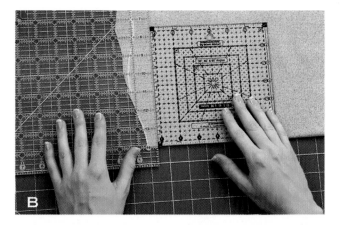

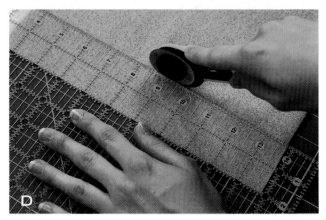

3. Place a large ruled square on the fabric so that its bottom edge is even with the fold of the fabric and the left side is approximately ½" from the uneven fabric end. Butt a long ruler against the left edge of the square *(Photo B)*. Remove the square but keep the long ruler in place.

4. Holding the ruler firmly in place, cut along the ruler's edge, trimming the uneven edge of the fabric *(Photo C)*. Exert firm, even pressure on the cutter as you roll it away from you.

Cutting Straight Strips. Straight, accurately cut strips are essential for quick piecing. Cut all strips across the 44" width of the fabric (selvage to selvage) unless instructed otherwise.

1. Position the ruler on the fabric at the squared-off edge, measuring the desired strip width from the edge of the fabric to the edge of the ruler *(Photo D)*. Cut through all layers, guiding the cutter along the edge of the ruler.

2. Check frequently to see that cuts remain perpendicular to the fold. If a strip is not cut at a true right angle to the fold, it will bow *(Photo E)*. If necessary, refold the fabric and square it up again to produce straight strips. Square up the ends of each strip and remove the selvages before cutting pieces.

Cutting Squares and Rectangles. Using a small ruler, such as a 6" x 12" or one specially designed for small cuts, align the desired measurement on the ruler with the strip end. Cut across the strip *(Photo F)*.

Cutting Half-Square Triangles. Half-square triangles are the most commonly used triangles in patchwork. The legs of a half-square triangle are on the straight of the grain, so the hypotenuse (diagonal edge) is on the bias. Corner triangles on diagonally-set quilts are half-square triangles.

1. Cut squares of fabric as stated in project instructions.

2. Cut each square in half diagonally to make two half-square triangles *(Photo G)*.

Cutting Quarter-Square Triangles. For a quarter-square triangle, the hypotenuse is on the straight of the grain and the legs are on the bias. This type of triangle is used when the long side of the triangle is the outer edge of a block or patchwork unit. Setting triangles at the sides of diagonally set quilts are quarter-square triangles.

1. Cut squares of fabric as stated in project instructions.

2. Cut each square in half diagonally in both directions to make four triangles *(Photo H)*—in other words, cut the square in an X.

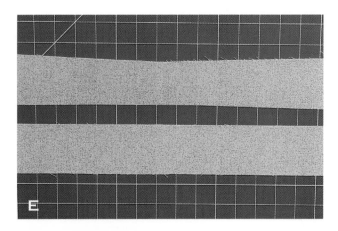

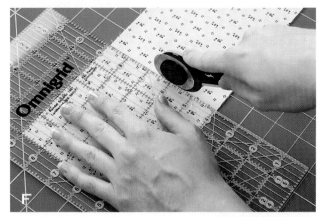

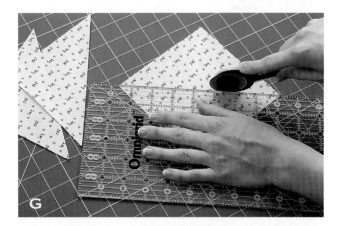

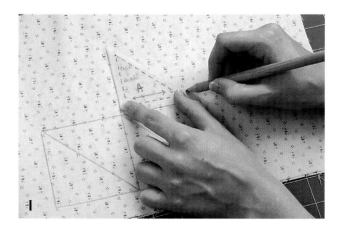

MACHINE PATCHWORK BASICS

The standard width for patchwork seams is ¼". If your seam width varies, the corners and points on your patchwork may not match and your project will turn out the wrong size. Before you begin, be sure that you can sew an accurate, consistent ¼" seam allowance.

TRADITIONAL MARKING AND CUTTING

1. Trace the pattern onto the plastic. Cut out the template with utility scissors.

2. For patchwork, mark around the template on the *wrong* side of the fabric *(Photo I)*. If your template includes ¼" seam allowances, cut each fabric piece on the drawn line. If your template is finished-size, allow space between the marked shapes. Add ¼" seam allowances around the shapes as you cut them from the fabric.

MEASURE THE SEAM

On many machines, the distance from the needle to the edge of the standard presser foot is exactly ¼". On some machines, you can move the needle to gauge a ¼" seam. If you can't move the needle or don't have a foot that accurately gauges ¼", invest in a patchwork presser foot that does.

If none of these options are available, add a masking tape seam guide to your throat plate as described here.

1. Use your rotary cutting ruler to mark a thin line ¼" from the edge of a piece of paper.

2. Put the paper under the presser foot and lower the needle through the line. Lower the foot and adjust the paper so that it is parallel with the edge of the foot *(Photo A)*.

3. Lay a strip of masking tape on the throat plate along the paper's edge. To make a raised seam guide, use a strip of moleskin (available in drug stores with foot care products).

Sew a Test Seam. Test your seam guide before starting a project. Set your machine to stitch 12–15 stitches per inch.

1. Cut two 3" squares of fabric. With right sides facing and edges aligned, join squares along one side. Press seam allowances to one side.

2. The combined width of the squares should be 5½". If your measurement is different, adjust your seam guide as needed to achieve a precise ¼" seam allowance.

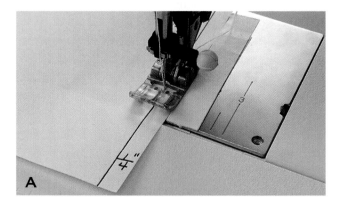

PRESSING AND PINNING

Always press a seam before crossing it with another seam. With right sides still facing, press the seam to set the stitches. Working from the right side, press seam allowances to one side.

Press seam allowances in opposite directions from row to row so that seams will oppose when joined *(Photo B)*. When possible, press seam allowances toward the darker of the two fabrics so that they will not show through the lighter fabric. We've suggested the direction to press seams in our step-by-step sewing instructions for each project.

Always press rather than iron. Lift the iron to move it, and press with an up-and-down motion. Sliding the iron back and forth can distort fabric. Concentrate on pressing seams rather than raw edges that might stretch.

Pinning. Rotary-cut strips and small patchwork units need not be pinned together before joining. For long seams, pin first at the ends, then the center, and along the length as needed. Place pins perpendicular to the seam line, with heads toward the fabric edge. If one piece is slightly longer than the other, distribute fullness evenly along the length of the seam and sew with the longer piece on the bottom so that the feed dogs can ease in the fullness *(diagram below)*.

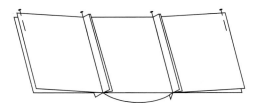

Pin Matching. Use pins to match seams when joining units. With right sides facing, align opposing seams. On the top piece, push a pin through the seam line ¼" from the top edge. Then insert the same pin into the seam of the bottom piece in the same manner *(Photo C)*. Set the pin, aligning seams. The joining seam should cross the point where the pin entered the fabric.

Sharp Points. When triangles or diamonds are joined, the seam lines cross in an X on the wrong side. Watch for this X as you sew these units to other units—if pinned correctly, the joining seam will go through the exact center of the X, and you will have nice sharp points on the front *(Photo D)*.

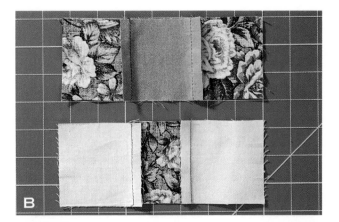

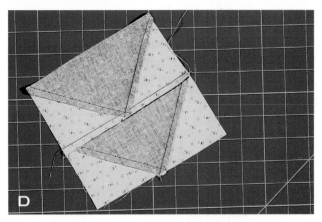

QUICK PIECING BASICS

Quick-piecing methods can be applied to the construction of many patchwork quilts. These methods have become standard in the repertoire of many quiltmakers today.

The patchwork quilts in this book were made using the techniques described here or with specialized methods that are explained with individual quilt instructions.

Begin a project by making one quick-pieced unit or strip set from scrap fabrics to learn how the techniques are applied. Then you will feel comfortable working assembly-line style with your chosen quilt fabrics.

STRIP PIECING

Cutting prejoined units from assembled strips is faster and often more accurate than traditional piece-by-piece sewing.

Sewing Strip Sets. A strip set is made of strips that are sewn together lengthwise in a particular sequence. Strip sets are later cut into segments to use as blocks or portions of blocks.

Time Saver!

Save time and thread by sewing chains of patchwork units, assembly-line style. When you have many of the same unit to sew, feed them through the machine one after another without cutting the thread. Backstitching is not necessary. As soon as one unit is stitched, feed in the next—the machine will make a few stitches before the needle strikes the next piece, creating a small thread chain. Carry the chain to the ironing board and snip units apart as you press them.

---

1. To make a strip set, pair two strips with right sides facing and raw edges aligned. Machine-stitch with a ¼" seam allowance *(Photo A)*. Add more strips as directed in the project instructions.

2. To press, begin by pressing strips flat, just as you have sewn them, to set the seam *(Photo B)*. Fold the top strip back, revealing the right side of the strip set. Press seam allowances to one side *(Photo C)*. After pressing, check to make sure that there are no folds or tucks along the seams.

A

B

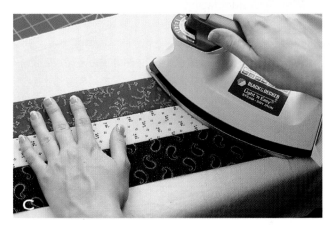

C

Cutting Strip Set Segments. Once the strip set is sewn and pressed, you will cut it into segments that become pre-assembled patchwork units.

1. With strip set extending to your left, align horizontal marks on the ruler with the long raw edges and seams of the strip set. Square up the uneven end of the strip set.

2. Turn the strip set around to cut. Keeping ruler lines parallel with the edges and seams of the strip set, measure and cut desired width segments *(Photo D)*.

DIAGONAL CORNERS

We used this method for several projects, such as *Farmer's Daughter.* It's an easy way to add triangle corners to a square or rectangle. Cutting and sewing are simplified since you cut squares for these pieces rather than triangles.

1. On the wrong side of the corner square, draw a diagonal line from corner to corner. If you prefer, you can press the square in half diagonally and use the crease for a stitching line. With practice, you'll be able to stitch small squares (up to 1½") by eye without having to mark a sewing line.

2. With right sides facing, match the corners of the square and base fabric (a square or rectangle). Stitch on the drawn line *(Diagram 1)*. Press the triangle open. Trim excess on both fabrics, leaving a ¼" seam allowance *(Diagram 2)*.

DIAGONAL ENDS

This method eliminates difficult measuring, cutting, and sewing of trapezoids. The technique is basically the same as for diagonal corners except a rectangle, instead of a square, is sewn to the corner of a base rectangle. We used this method for *Desert Mirage.*

1. With right sides facing, position the end rectangle perpendicular to the base fabric. Mark a diagonal line across the end rectangle in the same manner as for diagonal corners, beginning in the corner where the fabrics meet and angling toward the opposite corner of the *base rectangle* at a 45° angle *(Diagram 3)*.

2. Stitch on the marked line. Cut away excess fabrics from the corner seam allowance *(Diagram 4)*.

3. To make mirror-image diagonal ends *(Diagram 5)*, be careful to draw each sewing line in the correct direction.

Diagram 3

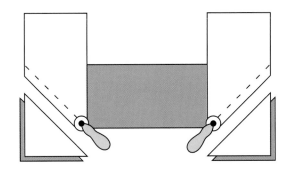

Diagram 4

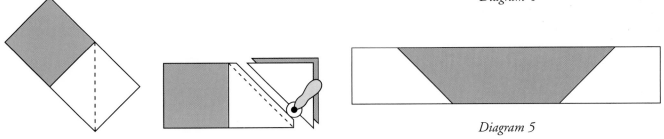

Diagram 5

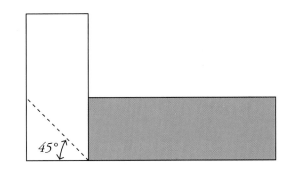

Diagram 1   *Diagram 2*

APPLIQUÉ

We used several techniques to make the appliqué quilts for this book. When making *String Star* and *Paper Dolls,* we fused appliqué pieces and then buttonhole-stitched around them by machine. Hand-buttonhole stitching, with no fusing, was used for the *Folk Art Stockings.* We used the machine again to create a look of hand appliqué for *Fancy Fans* and *Spring Blossoms.* These methods are great time-savers compared to traditional hand appliqué.

All appliqué patterns in this book are *finished* size. Depending on the appliqué method you choose, you may need to add seam allowances when cutting fabric pieces.

TRADITIONAL HAND APPLIQUÉ

For hand appliqué, make *finished-size* templates from plastic or freezer paper *(Photo A).* Trace plastic templates on the fabric's right side, allowing approximately ½" between tracings. Press freezer paper templates to the wrong side of the fabric. Cut out fabric pieces, adding approximately ³⁄₁₆" seam allowances *(Photo B).*

Turn under and hand-baste seam allowances before pinning pieces to the background fabric *(Photo C).* Or plan to roll edges under as you appliqué pieces.

Pin appliqué pieces to the background. Using sewing thread that matches the appliqué, make tiny slipstitches or blindstitches around each appliqué piece. Working from right to left, pull the needle through the background fabric and catch just a few threads along the fold of the appliqué *(Photo D).* Reinsert the needle into the background fabric directly next to where the last stitch ended and bring the needle up through the appliqué for the next stitch. Make stitches no farther than ⅛" apart.

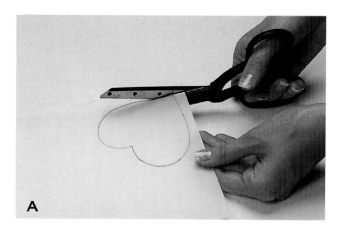

A

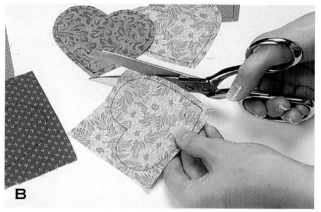

B

C

D

166

BUTTONHOLE APPLIQUÉ

Blanket- or buttonhole-stitch appliqué enjoyed great popularity between 1925 and 1940. The period style called for shapes to be secured and outlined with hand stitching in black thread. Quicker versions of this technique—using paper-backed fusible webbing and machine or hand stitching—are popular nowadays for making primitive-style quilts *(Photo E)*.

Cutting and Preparing Appliqués. Follow these steps to use fusible webbing to stabilize appliqués made from cotton fabric. Do not fuse wool appliqués.

1. Trace appliqué patterns onto paper (smooth) side of fusible webbing. You will need a separate tracing for each appliqué piece.

2. Rough-cut each shape, cutting slightly larger than drawn outline.

3. Following manufacturer's instructions, fuse web side of each piece to wrong side of appliqué fabric.

4. Cut out appliqués on drawn lines.

5. Peel off paper; then position appliqués on background fabric. Overlap pieces as needed.

6. Follow manufacturer's instructions to fuse appliqués to background fabric.

E

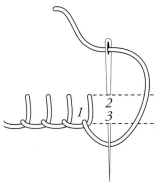

Buttonhole Stitch

Hand Stitching. Thread embroidery needle with floss or pearl cotton. Diagram at right shows how to make the buttonhole stitch. Use fewer strands of floss for delicate stitches and more strands for larger stitches. Hand-stitch around each piece, placing buttonhole stitches ⅛"–¼" apart.

Machine Stitching. Refer to your sewing machine manual for recommended machine settings. Sew some practice pieces and adjust stitch width and length as needed to achieve the desired effect. Set the machine so that no bobbin threads pull up to the top when stitching.

Stitch around appliqués, planning your sewing strategy to avoid stitching over previous stitches and making as few stops and starts as possible. The diagram included with the *Paper Dolls* instructions indicates the order and direction to sew. For *String Star*, each piece is machine-stitched in turn, leaving edges unsewn where they will be overlapped by another piece.

Additional Sewing Basket Supplies

❤ Paper-backed fusible webbing.

For hand stitching:
❤ Embroidery floss or pearl cotton to match or coordinate with appliqué fabrics.
❤ Hand-sewing embroidery needle.

For machine stitching:
❤ Sewing machine with blanket-stitch capability.
❤ Open-toed appliqué presser foot.
❤ Regular sewing thread or machine embroidery thread to match or coordinate with appliqué fabrics.

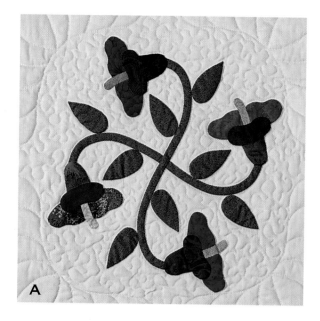

A

MOCK HAND APPLIQUÉ OR INVISIBLE MACHINE APPLIQUÉ

Machine appliqué done with monofilament nylon thread and a blindstitch or a small, open zigzag stitch imitates the look of hand appliqué. Marianne used this technique to make *Spring Blossoms (Photo A)*. Follow the steps below to prepare appliqués and to stitch them to background blocks.

Preparing Appliqué Pieces. Follow these instructions to make and apply a freezer-paper template for every appliqué piece in the quilt.

1. Trace patterns onto smooth (not shiny) side of freezer paper. Cut out paper templates on drawn lines. *Timesaving*

Additional Sewing Basket Supplies

- ❤ Fabric glue stick.
- ❤ Clear monofilament nylon thread, size .004.
- ❤ Two-ply cotton machine embroidery thread, size 60, in white or a color to match background fabric (regular sewing thread will do in a pinch).
- ❤ Size 60/8 or 70/10 sewing machine needles.
- ❤ Open-toed appliqué presser foot.
- ❤ Plastic-coated freezer paper.
- ❤ Tweezers.
- ❤ Spray water bottle.

Hint: Trace shapes as described. Stack additional sheets of freezer paper under tracing; staple together in a few places to prevent shifting. Cut several layers at a time.

2. Using a dry iron at wool setting, press shiny side of paper templates to *wrong* side of fabric, allowing approximately ½" between templates *(Photo B)*.

3. Cut out appliqué pieces, adding ³⁄₁₆" seam allowances around each shape. With small, sharp scissors, snip seam allowance at inside curves, clipping halfway to paper edge. This allows seam allowance to spread when turned so that curve will lie flat.

4. Apply fabric glue to the wrong side of each seam allowance. Use your fingers or a cool iron to fold seam allowances over the edges onto the paper side of the template and glue in place *(Photo C)*. Do not turn seam allowances that will be overlapped by another appliqué piece.

Setting Up Your Sewing Machine. Thread your machine on top with size .004 clear monofilament nylon thread. Use lightweight cotton machine-embroidery thread in the bobbin. Insert a size 60/8 or 70/10 needle and an open-toed embroidery presser foot.

Adjust your machine for either a short, narrow blindstitch or a narrow, fairly open, zigzag stitch. We find that the blindstitch is more invisible and we use it for relatively large pieces. A zigzag stitch seems to secure small pieces better. Refer to your sewing machine manual for suggested machine settings. Adjust the top tension so no bobbin threads pull up to the top when stitching.

Stitching. Before stitching any appliqués to the background, join pieces that overlap. (See *Paper Dolls* for an example of overlapping pieces that are joined first.) Then position all appliqués on the background fabric, pinning carefully *(Photo D)*.

Stitch appliqués in place, stitching right next to the folded edges. The left swing of the needle should just catch the folded edge and may catch a little of the paper underneath. Stitches should be approximately ⅛" apart. Backstitch a few stitches at the beginning and end to secure the threads.

After stitching, turn the block to the wrong side. Cut background fabric from behind the appliqués, leaving scant ¼" seam allowances. Moisten the fabric with a spray of water to dissolve the glue. Use tweezers to remove small paper pieces *(Photo E)*.

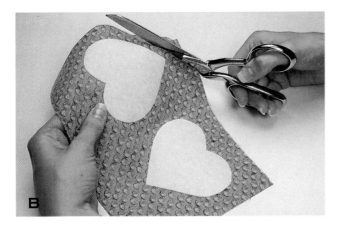

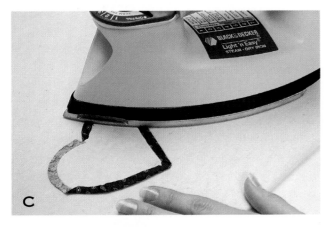

ASSEMBLING THE QUILT TOP

Instructions for the quilts in this book include steps for assembling the blocks, setting pieces, and borders to complete the quilt top.

JOINING BLOCKS

Our quilt assembly diagrams will help you arrange and construct rows. Join blocks into rows. Press seam allowances in alternate directions from row to row. Then join rows, pin-matching as needed before sewing. Press seam allowances to one side.

ADDING BORDERS

Border styles vary for the quilts in this book. Some are simple fabric borders. Others are pieced. Most have easy squared corners, but several have mitered borders.

To prepare your quilt top for borders, always measure through the middle of the quilt rather than along the edges, which might have stretched. Trim borders with square corners to correct size before sewing them to the quilt top. Wait to trim mitered borders until they are sewn to the quilt and corner seams are completed.

Borders with Mitered Corners. For multiple borders, first join border strips as directed to make border sets. Then follow mitering procedure below to join each border set to the quilt, treating each one as a single border.

1. Fold borders in half to find the center; press lightly to form a guideline. Draw a seam line with a ¼" allowance along the border's inner edge.

2. For side borders, measure along the seam line from the center guideline a distance equal to *half* the finished quilt length (or half the finished quilt width for top and bottom borders) and make a mark along the stitching line of the border. Repeat in the opposite direction (*Diagram 1*). Mark all four borders in this manner.

Press to form center guideline.

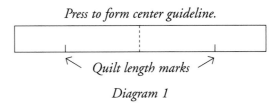

Quilt length marks

Diagram 1

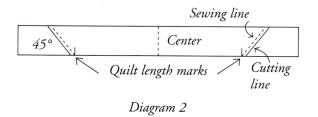

Sewing line

45° | *Center*

Quilt length marks | *Cutting line*

Diagram 2

3. Using a 45° angle on a 6" x 24" ruler as a guide, draw a 45°-angle line from each border end mark to the border's outer edge. This is the sewing line for the mitered corner. Mark a cutting line ¼" outside the sewing line *(Diagram 2)*. Do not cut excess border fabric until all border seams are completed.

4. With right sides facing and raw edges aligned, pin one border to the quilt, matching the border's center guideline to the quilt's center edge. Pin-match border end marks to finished corner points on the quilt top.

5. Sew the border to the quilt top between end pins only. Secure the seam with backstitches at each end. Sew all four borders to the quilt top in this manner.

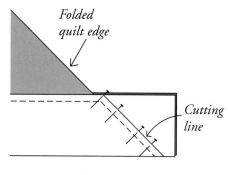

Folded quilt edge

Cutting line

Diagram 3

6. At one corner, pin-match marked sewing lines on adjacent borders, folding the quilt diagonally. Starting at the inner corner seam allowance, sew to the outside edge of the border *(Diagram 3)*. Secure the ends of the seam with backstitches. Repeat for all four corners.

7. Check seams to see that each corner lies flat and is square. Trim excess fabric from mitered seam, leaving ¼" seam allowances. Press seam allowances to one side.

READY TO QUILT

Much of your quilting can be done without marking. Outline quilting, whether in the ditch or ¼" from seams or appliqué edges, can be quilted "by eye." For straight-line machine quilting, you can use the edge of the presser foot or a special guide bar to space quilting evenly.

MARKING QUILTING DESIGNS

If quilting must be marked, do the marking before basting layers for quilting. Commercial quilting stencils are available in many different designs and are handy for marking intricate designs on any fabric *(Photo A)*.

To mark a quilting design from a pattern, trace it onto freezer paper. Darken lines with a permanent marker.

For fabrics light enough to see through, position the paper pattern under the quilt top and trace lines onto the fabric with a washable pencil such as an artist's silver pencil. For dark fabrics that you can't see through, use a large needle to punch holes in the paper pattern. With the pattern atop the quilt, mark through the holes, making small dots on the quilt top *(Photo B)*.

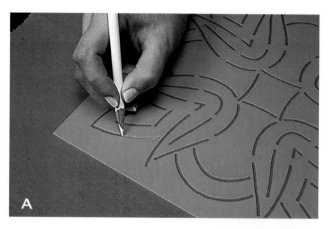

A

B

For simple quilting designs, such as stars or hearts, you can cut the shape from template plastic and mark around the edges *(Photo C)*.

Test Markers. Before using any marker on a quilt top, test to make sure the marks will wash out of the fabric. Mark on fabric scraps from the quilt and wash them in the sink or in the washer with other laundry.

MAKING THE QUILT BACK

Each materials list specifies the amount of 45"-wide fabric needed for backing. The project instructions explain how to divide the backing fabric and construct the quilt back. As an alternative, you can purchase wider fabric (54"–120" wide) for a seamless quilt back.

BATTING

We favor low-loft batting for our quilts. We like the flat, old-fashioned look of cotton or cotton/polyester batting. Manufacturers have made great improvements in batting products, so the new cotton and cotton-blend battings do not require the very close quilting that cotton batting did in the past. Read the information on the batting package before you use it in your quilt.

Cotton is certainly the batting of choice for machine quilters. Its reduced bulk makes a large quilt more manageable. Also, the quilt top and backing tend to cling to cotton, reducing puckers or pleats.

Before layering your quilt, unwrap the batting and let it breathe for a few hours to relax creases. You can tumble-dry some batts on low heat for five minutes to relax them.

LAYERING

Choose a large work surface where you can spread out the quilt—a large table, two tables pushed together, or a clean floor. We like to thread-baste for hand quilting and safety-pin baste for machine quilting.

Fold the backing in half lengthwise and lightly crease to create a center guideline. Fold the batting and quilt top in half and use straight pins to mark center guidelines.

Lay the quilt back right side down on the work surface. Use masking tape (or T-pins on carpet) to secure one long side of the quilt top to the work surface.

On the opposite side of the quilt back, tug gently to remove any wrinkles or folds; then tape or pin that edge to the work surface. Repeat for the two short ends. The back should be taut but not stretched out of shape.

Matching center marks, place the batting on the quilt back and smooth out wrinkles. Center the quilt top on the batting, right side up. The batting and backing should be approximately 3" larger than the quilt top on all sides.

Thread Basting. Using white thread and a long hand-sewing needle, begin basting at the center and work toward the outer edges. Baste with a zigzagging tailor's padding stitch, basting every 4"–5" *(Photo D)*.

If you plan to use a hoop for quilting, roll the backing and batting over on the outside edges and baste to protect the batting from tearing during quilting. Follow manufacturer's instructions if you are putting the quilt in a frame.

Safety-Pin Basting. Rustproof safety pins can be bought in bulk at most quilt and fabric shops. For a full-size quilt, you will need 500 to 700 1"-long pins.

Pin layers together, beginning at the center and working toward the edges. Pin every 4". Check spacing by placing your fist randomly on the quilt—the edges of your fist should touch pins. To avoid puckers, work from the top, pinning through all layers without reaching under the quilt.

HAND QUILTING

Hand-quilted stitches should be evenly spaced, with the spaces between stitches about the same length as the stitches themselves. The number of stitches per inch is less important than the uniformity of the stitching.

1. Place your work in a frame or hoop. Sit near good light and have your thimble, scissors, thread, and quilting needles at hand. Position yourself so that the line of quilting angles from upper right to lower left, so you can quilt toward yourself. (Reverse directions if you are left-handed.)

2. If you are new to quilting, choose a size 7 or 8 between. As your skill increases, use a smaller needle to make smaller stitches. Like fabric, thread has a grain, and working against the grain causes it to break easily. Thread the needle with about 18" of quilting thread *before* cutting the thread off the spool (so you will be going with the grain). Clip the thread from the spool. Make a small knot in the clipped end.

3. Insert the needle through the quilt top, 1" from the point where the quilting will start. Slide the needle through the top and batting, without piercing the backing, and bring it up at the beginning point. Pull the thread until the knot stops on the surface. Tug gently to pop the knot through the top into the batting. Use your thumbnail to encourage the knot through the fabric.

4. Insert the needle with the point straight down *(Photo A)*, about 1/16" from where the thread comes up. With your non-sewing hand under the quilt, feel for the point of the needle as it comes through the backing.

5. Push the fabric up from below as you rock the needle to a nearly horizontal position. Using the thumb of your sewing hand and the underneath hand, pinch a little hill in the fabric and push the tip of the needle back through the quilt top.

6. Rock the needle to an upright position to take another stitch before pulling it through. At first, load only three or four stitches on the needle *(Photo B)*. As you gain experience, try loading a few more stitches at a time.

7. End the line of quilting when you have about 6" of thread left. Tie a knot in the thread close to the quilt surface. Pop the knot through the top as before and clip the tail. Rethread the needle and continue quilting.

MACHINE QUILTING

Choose continuous-line quilting designs for machine quilting to minimize the number of times you must begin and end stitching.

PREPARING FOR MACHINE QUILTING

Adjust the tension so that the bobbin thread does not pull to the top. Set the needle to stop in the down position or try to stop stitching with the needle in the fabric.

Roll and fold the quilt if machine quilting a large quilt. Secure rolls with bicycle clips. You may prefer to leave the quilt open and drape it over your shoulder or hold it on your lap.

Extend your work area by setting up tables to the left and behind the machine to help support a large quilt while you are working.

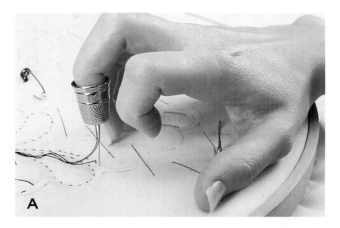

A

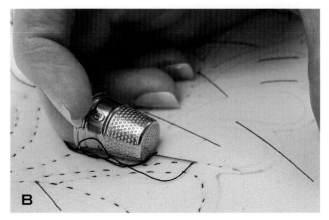

B

Additional Sewing Basket Supplies

- ❤ Sewing machine that lets you drop the feed dogs or cover them with a plate for free-motion quilting.
- ❤ Even-feed presser foot or walking foot for straight-line quilting.
- ❤ Darning or ring-type foot for free-motion quilting.
- ❤ For top thread, .004 monofilament nylon thread *or* regular sewing thread or machine-embroidery thread in a color that coordinates with the quilt fabrics.
- ❤ For bobbin thread, regular sewing thread in a color that blends with the backing fabric.
- ❤ Bicycle clips or machine quilting clips to keep the quilt rolled up while working.

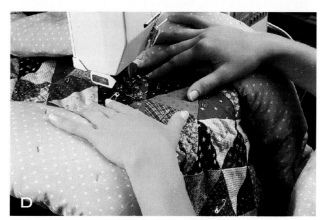

BEGINNING AND ENDING

Turn the hand wheel to take a stitch, pulling on the top thread to bring the bobbin thread to the surface *(Photo C)*. Hold onto both threads to prevent them from tangling when you begin quilting.

To secure thread ends at the beginning and end of quilting lines, make tiny, close stitches for about ¼".

QUILTING STRAIGHT LINES

Adjust the stitch length to 6–10 stitches per inch, or between 3 and 3.5 on some machines. Attach a walking foot to the machine.

Use your hands to assist the walking foot as you quilt *(Photo D)*. Spread the fabric slightly with your hands and gently push fabric toward the foot to prevent puckering and reduce the drag on the fabric.

FREE-MOTION QUILTING

Free-motion machine quilting is a skill you must practice in order to master. Start with small projects that are easy to manipulate. Concentrate on following the design—smooth, even stitches will come with practice. Do not become discouraged if your first try is less than perfect.

1. Attach a darning foot or free-motion quilting foot; then lower the feed dogs or cover them. No stitch length

adjustment is necessary; you will control the stitch length by manually moving the fabric.

2. Rest fingertips on fabric, with a hand on each side of the presser foot so you can move the fabric freely and evenly. To make even stitches, run the machine at a steady, medium speed and move the fabric smoothly and evenly so that the needle follows the design *(Photo E)*. Do not rotate the quilt; simply move the fabric forward, backward, and side to side.

BINDING

Our favorite quilt binding is a double-layered French-fold binding. The double layer wears well and is easy to make and apply. To prevent puckers from forming as you sew binding to the quilt edge, an even-feed or walking foot is helpful.

MAKING STRAIGHT-GRAIN BINDING

We use straight-grain binding to finish most quilts. For quilts with rounded corners or curved edges such as *Fancy Fans*, use bias binding since it has more stretch. See the tip box on page 18 for instructions for making continuous bias for binding.

1. Cut the designated number of crossgrain fabric strips. (You should get approximately 40" of usable length from each strip.) We cut 2"-wide strips when we use cotton or other thin batting and 2¼"-wide strips for thicker polyester battings.

2. Join strips end-to-end to make a continuous strip that is the length specified in the project instructions. To join two strips, layer them perpendicular to each other with right sides facing. Then stitch a diagonal seam across the strips. Trim seam allowance to ¼" *(Photo A)*. Press seam allowances open.

3. With wrong sides facing, fold binding in half along the length of the strip and press *(Photo B)*.

APPLYING BINDING WITH MITERED CORNERS

Binding is sewn to the front of the quilt first. Begin stitching in the middle of any quilt side.

1. Leave approximately 4" of the binding strip free when you begin stitching. Aligning raw edges of binding with the quilt top edge, stitch through all layers with a ¼"-wide seam.

2. Stop stitching ¼" from the quilt corner and backstitch. Remove the quilt from the machine *(Photo C)*. *Hint:* Placing a pin at the ¼" point will remind you where to stop stitching.

3. Rotate the quilt a quarter turn. Fold the binding straight up, away from the corner, making a 45°-angle fold *(Photo D)*.

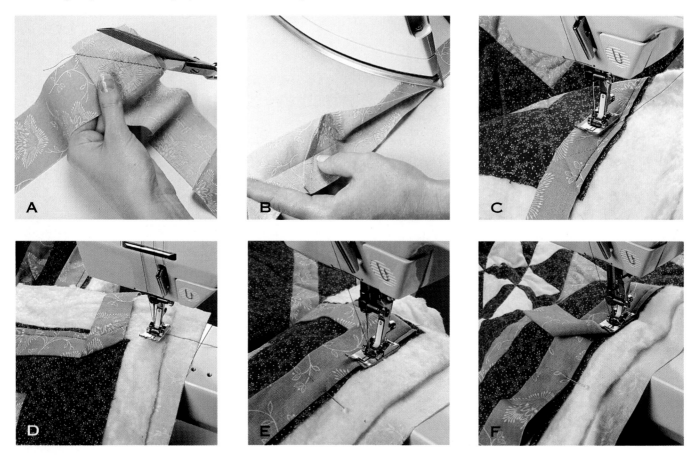

SIGNING YOUR QUILT

Signing and dating your quilt is an important step in finishing it. Think of the signature patch as a diary of your quilt's history. We like to add information such as the occasion for which the quilt was made, the length of time it took to make, and the recipient of the quilt.

Cut a muslin square the size you want the signature patch to be and a matching square of plastic-coated freezer paper. Use a dry, warm iron to adhere the shiny side of the paper to the wrong side of the muslin to stabilize it while writing.

Use a fine-tip permanent pen such as a Micron Pigma™ to write on fabric. Peel off the paper. Turn under seam allowances around the patch and hand-stitch it to the quilt back.

Another easy way to write on paper-backed muslin is to roll it into a typewriter and type an inscription onto the fabric.

Embroidery and cross-stitch can also be used to make lovely signature patches.

This quilt was made by the staff and friends of the Buckner (MO) Elementary School to be presented to

Caroline Overton

upon her retirement
June 2, 1988

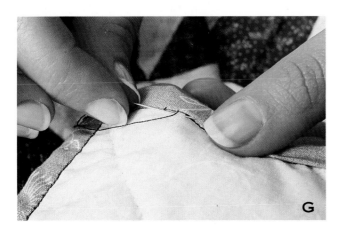

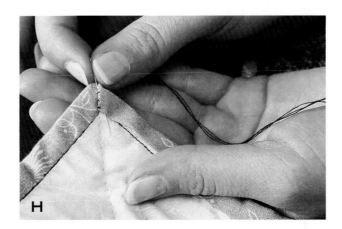

4. Bring binding straight down in line with the next edge, leaving the top fold even with the raw edge of the previously sewn side. Begin stitching at the top edge, sewing through all layers *(Photo E)*. Stitch all corners in this manner.

5. Stop stitching as you approach the beginning point. Fold the 4" tail of binding back over on itself and pin *(Photo F)*. The end of the binding should overlap this folded section. Continue stitching through all layers

½"–1" beyond the folded tail. Trim extra binding. (When turned back, the fold conceals the raw end of the binding.)

6. Trim excess batting and quilt back even with seam allowance.

7. Turn binding over seam allowance to quilt back. Blind-stitch fold to backing fabric *(Photo G)*.

8. At corners, fold binding to miter and blindstitch along diagonal fold *(Photo H)*.

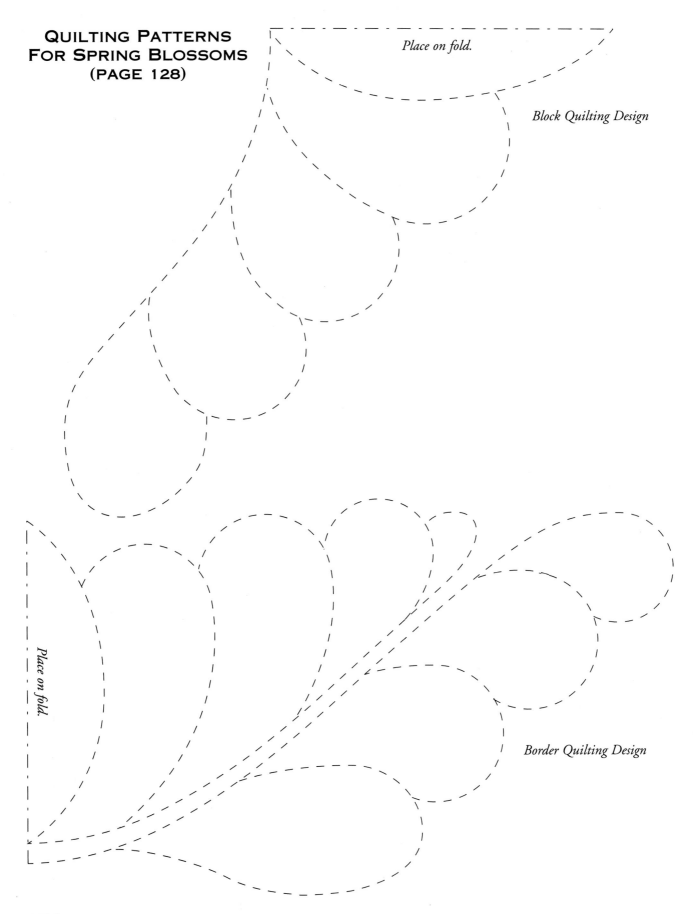

**QUILTING PATTERNS
FOR SPRING BLOSSOMS**
(PAGE 128)

Place on fold.

Block Quilting Design

Place on fold.

Border Quilting Design

176